Feeling Pain and Being in Pain

Feeling Pain and Being in Pain

second edition

Nikola Grahek

A Bradford Book
The MIT Press
Cambridge, Massachusetts
London, England

MIT Press books may be purchased at special quantity discounts for business or sales promotional use. For information, please email special_sales@mitpress.mit.edu or write to Special Sales Department, The MIT Press, 55 Hayward Street, Cambridge, MA 02142.

This book was set in Stone serif and Stone sans by SNP Best-set Typesetter Ltd., Hong Kong, and was printed and bound in the United States of America.

Library of Congress Cataloging-in-Publication Data

Grahek, Nikola.
 Feeling pain and being in pain / by Nikola Grahek.—2nd ed.
   p. ; cm.
"A Bradford book."
Includes bibliographical references and index.
ISBN-13: 978-0-262-07283-0 (hardcover : alk. paper)
1. Pain. 2. Pain perception. I. Title.
[DNLM: 1. Pain. 2. Pain Threshold. WL 704 G742f 2007]

RB127.G727 2007
616'.0472—dc22

                              2006030376

10 9 8 7 6 5 4 3 2 1

Contents

For Ana, Ivan, and Nela

Acknowledgments

This book was conceived and written while I was fellow of the Hanse-Wissenschaftskolleg (Hanse Institute for Advanced Study) in Delmenhorst, Germany. I am grateful to the Rector of Hanse Institute, Gerhard Roth, for support, encouragement, and understanding. My special thanks go to my host, Hans Flohr, for his interest, friendship, and the fruitful discussions we had. I am indebted to the staff of the Hanse Institute and to all Fellows for the wonderful time that I had during my twelve months' stay. I am particularly grateful to Mechthild Harders-Opolka and to Uwe Opolka for their friendship and support. For long-term support and lasting interest in my work I am indebted to Daniel Dennett, Boris Velichkovsky, Jay Rosenberg, David Rosenthal, Helmut Hildebrandt, Peter Bieri, Milos Arsenijevic, Zivan Lazovic, Jovan Arandjelovic, and Leon Kojen.

Foreword

In the headlong scramble by psychologists, neuroscientists, and many others to understand the mind these days, what roles can philosophers usefully play? Many of the perplexities that bedevil researchers are philosophical in one important sense: we don't even know whether we are asking the right questions. But are philosophers any better than scientists at repairing and then answering these ill-posed questions? What is the likelihood that philosophers' training, scholarship, habits of thought, and talent actually equip them well for making progress instead of wallowing unproductively in a swamp of disputes, rebuttals, and fancy footwork going nowhere? Sad to say, much of what philosophers have to say about the mind these days is wisely ignored by serious researchers, but there is a fast growing cadre of philosophers of cognitive science or neurophilosophers who are well poised to contribute to the solution or resolution of these problems, and Nikola Grahek was one of these, leading the way for others before his untimely death at the end of September 2003. He had both the conceptual acuity of a well-trained philosopher and an intimate, broad-based knowledge of the empirical science relating to his chosen topic: pain. Putting the two together, and proceeding in a constructive, optimistic spirit, he came up with some startling and attention-shifting proposals about how to make sense of pain, revisionary proposals that should clarify the thinking of scientist and layperson alike.

At first glance, the idea that there is an important difference between feeling pain and being in pain does not ring many bells. Isn't it some sort of *conceptual* truth that when you are in pain you feel it, and when you feel it, you are in it? Perhaps, but then the concepts that constitute that conceptual truth may need to be revised or discarded. This possibility is all but invisible to traditional philosophers of mind and to the champions of the recent (regressive) turn to "analytic metaphysics," a descendant of the ordinary language philosophy of the 1950s and '60s. These philosophers assume that subjecting our everyday concepts of mental phenomena—consciousness, pain, sensation, intention, etc.—to rigorous conceptual analysis yields a priori truths about mental phenomena, truths that must anchor or constrain all empirical work on them. The prospect that our everyday concepts might prove to be subtly unfit, unable to bear the weight of scientific discovery, is largely ignored. The results, however brilliant, are thus best seen as a variety of blinkered auto-anthropology, an articulation of *the world of the Anglophone layperson*. This is a fine place to *start*, and Grahek displays a keen philosophical appreciation of the nuances in our everyday concepts of pain, but then he takes on the much more challenging—and much more interesting!—task of trying to put the fruits of that analysis into registration with what we have learned about pain in the clinic and laboratory.

There are many counterintuitive findings in the empirical literature on pain, and philosophers who live by their intuitions stumble badly when they breezily assume that no philosophically relevant facts could be hiding from them. This book is an excellent port of entry into that world, and should be required reading for all would-be philosophers of mind. Empirical researchers will also find here a calm, clear illumination of the conceptual fogs and shadows that can bedevil their own thinking about what they have observed. Anyone who has thought hard about pain knows that it can seem impossibly paradoxical and cryptic. Deciphering the many manifestations is a multi-disciplinary task, and Grahek has provided a framework for unifying our morsels of understanding into a single perspective.

Nikola Grahek died in Belgrade a few days after sending in the final revisions of this revised edition of his monograph, first published in *Hanse-Studien* (in English) in 2001. I learned of his death as I was drafting this foreword, and my anguish on realizing that because of my procrastination he would not get to read this was tempered by my recognition that he already knew how highly I regarded his work. I founded the Center for Cognitive Studies at Tufts in 1985, and over nearly two decades it has hosted a remarkable series of researchers, most of them philosophers and all of them philosophically acute, who have had in common the belief that there is an important role for informed philosophers to play in the development of good scientific theories of mental phenomena. I am particularly proud of our alumni: Kathleen Akins, Nicholas Humphrey, Evan Thompson, and Alva Noë are no doubt the best known so far, but don't be surprised to see major contributions in the near future from the others (whose details can be found on the Center's website, at http://www.ase.tufts.edu/cogstud/). Of none am I more proud than Nikola Grahek.

I first met Nikola at the Zentrum für Interdiziplinäre Forschung (ZIF) in Bielefeld, Germany, in 1990, when he came from his native Belgrade, then Yugoslavia, to participate in the famously productive international mind–brain research group that met there during that year. In 1994–95, when Belgrade was plunged into chaos and poverty, I invited him to bring his family to Boston and spend a year at Tufts as my Research Associate at the Center for Cognitive Studies, where he continued his research on pain and participated with me in the early exploratory discussions on how to create the architecture of Cog, Rodney Brooks's pioneering humanoid robot project at MIT's AI Lab. I remember vividly the tutorial on the different roles of pain that he gave for the assembled graduate students who were then thinking about how to implement a pain system in the robot. At the end of the year, he and his family had to return to a scarcely improved situation in Belgrade, where he continued his work under appalling conditions. When his monograph first appeared in the German series *Hanse-Studien* (Delmenhorst, 2001) I decided to include it in the required reading for a seminar I was offering at Tufts on scientific and philosophical problems of consciousness. It made an unusually large contribution to that seminar, and since the reaction of my students was so positive, I decided that this work should be brought to a wider audience. Grahek's English was very good, and very clear, but occasionally marred by the awkwardnesses and misdirections that are well nigh inevitable in a work outside one's native tongue, so I commissioned two of my graduate students, Lindsay Beyerstein and Valentina Urbanek, who both had a deep understanding of the text, to copy edit it with an eye to smoothing the occasional rough edges and clarifying the sometimes quite complex trains of thought one must follow to see what Grahek is saying and what he is not saying. It was their proposed revisions that Nikola was reviewing when illness struck so cruelly.

Nikola and his family had survived the trauma of the terrible Milošević years and emerged into the bright and promising future that is now unfolding in Serbia and Montenegro. When my wife and I visited them in Belgrade in June of 2002, we were thrilled to find that life was improving dramatically after the ousting of Milošević, and at last Nikola could hope to pass on the fruits of his researches to students worthy of them, at the University of Belgrade. He will not be able to enjoy this transmission of his discoveries in person, but thanks to MIT Press, his influence will continue, and grow. He has set a fine example for young philosophers to follow.

Daniel Dennett
Tufts University

1 Introduction

This book is principally devoted to the thorough consideration and general theoretical appreciation of the two most radical dissociation syndromes to be found in human pain experience. The first syndrome is characterized by the complete dissociation of the sensory dimension of pain from its affective, cognitive, and behavioral components. The second syndrome is an absolute dissociation in the opposite direction: the total dissociation of the pain experience's affective components from its sensory-discriminative components. The former syndrome can be described as *pain without painfulness* and the latter as *painfulness without pain*. In the first case, one is able to feel pain but is not able to be in pain, whereas in the second case one is able to be in pain but is not able to feel pain. Given our common experience of pain, it might seem to us that the two syndromes just described are inconceivable and, thus, impossible. In order to make them more intelligible and, thus, less inconceivable, I will explain the crucial distinction between *feeling pain* and *being in pain,* and defend it on conceptual and empirical grounds. But the main point is that we know that *pain without painfulness* and *painfulness without pain* are, however bizarre or outlandish, nonetheless possible for the simple reason that clinical evidence amply documents their existence. So, the question is not whether they exist or could exist, but what they can teach us about the true nature and structure of human pain experience. Accordingly, the major theoretical aim of this book will be to appreciate what lessons are to be learned from these syndromes as far as our very concept, or more importantly, our very experience of pain is concerned.

The first lesson is that although pain appears to be a simple, homogenous experience, it is actually a complex experience comprising sensory-discriminative, emotional-cognitive, and behavioral components. These components are normally linked together, but they can become disconnected and therefore, much to our astonishment, they can exist separately. The second lesson is that pain, once deprived of all its affective, cognitive, and behavioral components, loses all of its representational and motivational force: it is no longer a signal of threat or injury, and it no longer moves one's mind or body in any way. The third lesson is that pain deprived of its sensory-discriminative components comes to such sensory indeterminacy that it cannot be distinguished from other unpleasant sensations, or sensations of other quality, and loses all informational power with regard to the location, intensity, temporal profile, and nature of harmful stimuli. Thus, the two most radical dissociation syndromes of human pain experience may reveal the truly complex nature of pain—its major constitutional elements, the proper role these play in overall pain experience, and the way they work together, as well as the basic neural structures and mechanisms that subserve them.

Pain without painfulness is found in patients who suffer from a rare neurological syndrome known as *pain asymbolia*. Characteristically, these patients feel pain upon harmful stimulation, but their pain no longer represents danger or threat to them. These patients do not mind pain at all; indeed, they may even smile or laugh at it. But as I will try to show, this pain that doesn't represent any threat or danger to the *subject* is a dire threat to both the subjectivist and the objectivist conceptions or interpretations of pain. This anomalous syndrome threatens the subjectivist view that the sensation of pain, that is, its distinctive phenomenal content or quality—the "what-it-is-likeness" of pain—is the essential component of our total pain experience and plays the central or fundamental role in it. Pain asymbolia also threatens the objectivists' claim that the feeling of pain is just the awareness of an objective bodily state of affairs: that it is the perception or sensory representation of bodily or tissue damage. Actually, the consideration of pain asymbolia might help us to appreciate the strengths and weaknesses of the subjectivist and objectivist conceptions of pain. In other words, it might help us to see the proper role of pain sensation or pain quality in overall pain experience. It might also help us understand how pain represents bodily damage and threats to physical well-being.

Pain asymbolia, or pain without painfulness, is in yet another conceptual and theoretical respect important for the proper understanding of human pain experience. This syndrome is unique among the reactive dissociation syndromes of human pain experience. As I will try to show, it is to be regarded as the only clear-cut case in which severe pain is not experienced as unpleasant, and in which there are no traces of any other aversive attitude toward it. Pain asymbolia is the only condition that produces complete, thoroughgoing indifference to pain. This syndrome is uniquely distinguished by the absence of any appropriate pain behavior, or any tendency or disposition toward such behavior. But owing to its purity and simplicity, the case of pain asymbolia is also the most perspicuous example of pain that has lost all its biological function and significance: it is recognized by the subject as pain and is felt as located in certain body parts. But it means nothing to him and is at most something that he laughs or smiles at. Bentham wrote that Nature has placed humankind "under the governance of two sovereign masters: *pain and pleasure*" (1948, p. 1). But which pain? What part of pain? How does pain exert power over humankind?

To answer these questions, we have to look more closely at the biological significance and function of pain. The opening chapter of this book is devoted to the consideration of exactly these issues. My analysis of the biological significance and function of pain, as well as my inquiry into the true nature and structure of pain through the study of dissociation phenomena in human pain experience, will always be grounded on the consideration of the basic neural structures and mechanisms that subserve and are responsible for pain experience. But at some point the "hard" problems of consciousness will come into play. The "hard" problems concern the very intelligibility of the connection between the experience of pain, as an eminently subjective or phenomenal state, and the activity of the corresponding neural structures and mechanisms: Why does this neural activity give rise to the sensation of pain and not to some other sensation? Why does it give rise to any sensations at all? The closing chapter of the book is dedicated to the consideration of these intelligibility issues. I will claim that the phenomenal or subjective state of pain and the neural structures responsible for its appearance share one property that makes their connection intelligible. Once this common property is perceived, we will only have to apply the simple hermeneutical injunction: *just connect the subjective state with the neural structure.* However, my theoretical ambition is not to solve the "hard" problems of consciousness as they relate to the experience of pain; I merely seek to lift some of the burden that hangs around them.

Before I take up any of these considerations, I have to make one more remark about the major theoretical intentions of this book. Throughout the book, from the very beginning to the very end, I do my best to resist the strong philosophical temptation to prejudge on the basis of preconceived ideas whether *pain without painfulness* and *painfulness without pain* should be treated as cases of pain at all. It is more interesting and important to learn something from these bizarre and puzzling cases about the true nature and structure of pain, than to relish the fact that another piece of evidence speaks in favor of one's cherished theory, or to despair if it does not. In other words, in this book the reader will not find another philosophical theory of pain that is supposed to conclusively support or definitely refute the deeper metaphysical, semantic, and epistemological intuitions that lie behind subjectivism or objectivism in the philosophy of mind. The main theoretical or philosophical ambition of the book is a more modest one: to appreciate the strengths and weaknesses of these intuitions and thereby to show that a less doctrinaire and more balanced approach to the study of mind–brain phenomena is quite salutary and, indeed, highly recommendable. At this stage of pain research and theory, we still do not have a fully satisfactory conceptual and neural model of pain that would explain all puzzling phenomena to be found in human pain experience and put pain under firm control. However, we do know much more about pain than we knew only a few decades ago. We have a much better and broader insight into the major biological and psychological mechanisms that are vitally important to the survival and protection of humankind, not to mention animals. If this book is appreciated by its readers as a modest contribution to such insight, it will definitely serve—to the author's great satisfaction—its major purpose.

2 The Biological Function and Importance of Pain

The capacity to feel pain upon harmful external stimulation or upon internal bodily damage is certainly the most precious gift bestowed on us by Mother Nature for self-protective purposes. However, those who are lucky enough to be able to feel pain when their bodies are exposed to damaging (or potentially damaging) stimuli have highly ambivalent or even paradoxical attitudes toward that gift. This attitude is best captured by the title of Brand and Yancey's (1997) book, *The Gift Nobody Wants*. For it is true that, when in pain, we dislike it very much, and will do anything to get rid of it or at least alleviate it, especially if the pain is intrusive or severe. However, when not in pain, we are certainly grateful for that precious gift handed to us by Mother Nature. A moment's reflection will convince us of the threat to the integrity of our bodies and minds that would ensue if we were deprived of it by disease or congenital defect. The most dramatic and frightening evidence comes from the consideration of people who suffer from so-called *congenital analgesia*, the first case of which is said to have been reported by Dearborn (1932). His patient made a living as a human pincushion. Once, his crucifixion act had to be called off when a woman in the audience fainted after a spike was driven through his hand. But the best-documented of all cases of congenital analgesia is the case of Miss C., a young Canadian student at McGill University in Montreal:

As a child, she had bitten off the tip of her tongue while chewing food, and has suffered third-degree burns after kneeling on a hot radiator to look out of the window. When examined . . . she reported that she did not feel pain when noxious stimuli were presented. She felt no pain when parts of her body were subjected to strong electric shock, to hot water at temperatures that usually produce reports of burning pain, or to prolonged ice-bath. . . . A variety of other stimuli, such as inserting a stick up through the nostrils, pinching tendons, or injections of histamine under the skin—which are normally considered as forms of torture—also failed to produce pain.

Miss C. had severe medical problems. She exhibited pathological changes in her knees, hip and spine, and underwent several orthopedic operations. Her surgeon attributed these changes to the lack of protection to joints usually given by pain sensation. She apparently failed to shift her weight when standing, to turn over in her sleep, or to avoid certain postures, which normally prevent the inflammation of joints.

All of us quite frequently stumble, fall or wrench a muscle during ordinary activity. After these trivial injuries, we limp a little or we protect the joint so that it remains unstressed during the recovery process. This resting of the damaged area is an essential part of its recovery. But those who feel no pain go on using the joint, adding insult to injury. (Melzack and Wall 1988, pp. 4–5)

Paul Brand has frequently observed this stunning behavior, and its disastrous consequences, among his leprosy patients in the land called "the land of painlessness." Leprosy bacilli destroy the peripheral nociceptors, the specialized sensors that respond to damaging or potentially damaging stimuli and evoke pain sensation. Leprosy bacilli thrive in the cooler peripheral parts of the body, such as the digits and the nose, while sparing the warmer areas like the armpits and the groin. The disease leaves the extremities numb, and thus completely unprotected from injuries which do not seem to bother the patients at all. As Brand noticed, half of the problem with leprosy patients is painlessness. Brand was struck by the absolute carelessness of leprosy patients toward their injuries, and their lack of attempts to protect their damaged body parts from further injury. He recalls the case of a young boy who worked in the weaving shops of the leprosy sanatorium. The young weaver was working vigorously at a loom, probably showing off for the director and his guest, when Brand spotted traces of blood on the cotton cloth:

"May I see your hand?" I yelled to the weaver. . . . He held out a deformed, twisted hand with shortened fingers. The index finger had lost maybe a third of an inch in length, and as I looked closer I saw naked bone protruding from a nasty, septic wound. This boy was working with a finger cut to the bone!

"How did you cut yourself?" I asked. He gave a nonchalant reply: "Oh, it's nothing. I had a pimple on my finger, and earlier it bled a little. I guess it's opened up again." (Brand and Yancey 1997, p. 89)

Deprived of the ability to feel pain from noxious or potentially noxious stimuli, Miss C. and Brand's leprosy patients were deprived of Nature's most sophisticated and efficient self-protective psychophysical system—with disastrous consequences. This system normally serves as a reliable alarm mechanism that warns the organism about harmful or potentially harmful features of its environment. This system also monitors the extent of the damage inflicted. Finally it induces the organism to take evasive action, or to refrain from doing anything that might exacerbate the damage. At the most basic level, "the" pain system actually consists of two subsystems: (1) the avoidance system and (2) the restorative or repair system. In more picturesque terms, the first might be called the *external pathologist,* and the second the *internal pathologist.* Although both subsystems function as alarm or warning systems, they differ markedly in their functions, targets, and underlying neural structures and mechanisms, as well as in the characteristic behavior that they induce. In order to survive and preserve their vital physical and mental capacities, organisms must *avoid* threats and *protect* themselves from destructive stimuli. Finally, when they are hurt, they must be able to *guard* their injuries against further insult. The first two protective functions are carried out by the avoidance system, while the third is performed by the restorative or repair system. (Until recently, protective pain mechanisms were largely neglected in pain research and evolutionary theory.)

The *avoidance system* is sensitive to noxious (or potentially noxious) mechanical, thermal, and chemical stimuli. Potentially noxious stimuli are those which, if prolonged, would damage body tissue. (For the sake of brevity, I will use the term "noxious" to include both immediately and potentially dangerous stimuli.) A system that can reliably detect noxious stimuli and induce immediate withdrawal has a powerful and sophisticated *preventive* capacity; and this capacity has great protective and survival value. For example, this system must respond to temperatures just below 48°C, the threshold above which nerve damage occurs. The system must also respond to the pressure of a thorn or a needle just below the force sufficient to break the skin.

We know a fair amount about the neural basis of the avoidance system. Intraneural microrecording and microstimulation experiments have demonstrated that humans and other species have neural structures that respond preferentially to noxious stimuli. Such physiologically specialized neural structures include the "fast" A-Δ nerve fibers[1] and the "slow" C-fibers. Impulses travel along A-Δ fibers at 6 to 30 m/s, whereas C-fibers transmit only at 0.5 to 1.5 m/s. This means that it can take more than a second for the nerve impulses conducted by C-fibers to reach the spinal cord from an injured foot, while the nerve impulses transmitted by A-Δ fibers from the same part of the body reached it long before. Qualitatively speaking, the excitation of A-Δ nociceptive fibers corresponds to fast, sharp, pricking pain (first pain, or alarm pain), whereas the activity of C-nociceptive fibers is related to slow, dull, or burning pain (second pain, or to speculate a bit, remembrance pain). Both types of pain convey precise information about the location of the insult. Their function appears to be reserved for pain "as a signal of noxious challenge to the body surface which needs to be well localized for the purposes of removal of agent, protection of the injured site, or inhibition by gentle rubbing or scratching" (Ochoa and Torebjörk 1989, p. 593). This is the main reason why the avoidance system is known as the "external pathologist." Physiologically, the activation of A-Δ nociceptive and C-nociceptive fibers is strongly connected to withdrawal reflexes, such as the flexion reflex and the corneal reflex. Behaviorally, their activity is followed by positive bodily reactions: movement and manipulation. From the biological point of view, the avoidance system is primarily a surface, skin-protective system—the skin being the part of the body that is most frequently exposed to noxious stimuli. Finally, from the

1. A-Δ fibers are small, fast-conducting myelinated fibers with high activation thresholds. Unmyelinated C-fibers are small, polymodal, and slow-conducting fibers (conductive velocity 0.5 to 1.5 m/sec) (Price and Dubner 1977; Wall and McMahon 1985; Torebjörk, Vallbo, and Ochoa 1987; Ochoa and Torebjörk 1989).

clinical point of view, it is useful to know that the avoidance system tends to evoke transient pain in response to minor insults. However, it may also be associated with early acute pain stemming from frank damage to the body tissue:

The alerting function of acute pain reflects the phasic activation of sensors (nociceptors) by potentially dangerous stimuli exceeding the physiological range. This warning purpose of pain is most evident as concerns skin, which is exposed to external dangers. Acute, cutaneous pain evokes, thus, motor withdrawal and/or "flight" reaction, protective responses intended to discontinue exposure to the noxious stimulus and, thereby, to terminate the pain. (Millan 1999, p. 7)

Through a simple psychophysical self-experiment, you can easily test the qualitative, temporal, and spatial differences between the painful sensations evoked by the activity of your A-Δ and C-nociceptive fibers. This experiment will help you appreciate how finely these nerves are tuned to detect potentially dangerous conditions which would otherwise cause serious injury. First, hold your fingertip, which is of moderately normal sensitivity to temperature, very close to a hot electric light bulb for two seconds. Then press it against the light bulb, keep it there for a second, and then remove it quickly—which you will do anyway because it will be very painful. During the first two seconds you are going to feel a diffuse (nonpainful) sensation of heat that is not related to the activity of your nociceptors, but rather stems from the stimulation of A-β thermo-receptors. Then, near the end of the third second or just before the spontaneous removal of your fingertip from the light bulb, you will suddenly experience the short-lived, stinging or pricking pain in a punctuate location. This pain is evoked by the activity of your A-Δ heat nociceptors because the stimulus has become potentially noxious. This sensation will be followed, after a brief interval, by a longer-lasting sensation of intense heat and burning pain whose appearance is due to the activity of C-polymodal nociceptors. Normally, A-Δ heat nociceptors would have started to respond just before the contact temperature reached damaging levels. The stinging pain would normally cause you to withdraw your finger. The stinging pain elicited via A-Δ heat nociceptive fibers is a message that the thermal stimulus has become potentially dangerous. If you had not removed your fingertip instantly from the hot light bulb, it would have been burned. This happened to me once when I, quite unwisely, and out of sheer theoretical curiosity, left my fingertip on the hot light bulb too long. I got burned and a blister developed, staying on my sore finger for almost a month. This would not have happened if I had taken seriously the simple message of my A-Δ heat nociceptive fibers, sent to me via stinging pain: that the thermal stimulus was potentially dangerous; that it was a threat to the integrity of my body and my mind. But this is not the only role that pain played in the hurtful story of my initial foolishness. Fortunately, once the damage was done—the long-lasting blister developed—the restorative or repair pain system came into play.

The restorative system is sensitive to lasting changes produced by damage to the joints, muscles, and nerves. It reacts by inhibiting movement and manipulation of the affected areas. This is the rationale for labeling it the "internal pathologist." The restorative system prevents the organism from inflicting further insults to the already damaged areas of the body. Neurophysiologically, it is subserved by "silent" C-nociceptive chemo-fibers. These fibers do not respond immediately to noxious stimuli, not even to excessive ones. Instead they react to chemicals released after the injury has been inflicted

(McMahon and Koltzenburg 1990, pp. 254–255). The system is slow—the transportation of neurotransmitters proceeds at a rate of only 224 millimeters per 24 hours—but is of lasting and steady influence. Activation of the restorative system is usually followed by tenderness (primary and secondary hyperalgesia and hyperesthesia) which spreads around the damaged part of the joint, muscle, or nerve, making it sensitive even to completely innocuous stimuli. From the biological point of view, the state produced by this system "has the function of greatly diminishing movement or manipulation. Even though it may be annoying, it is the optimal condition to speed recovery from deep injury" (Melzack and Wall 1988, p. 107). Consider how infants and animals react to severe injury and the healing process, and compare it to the obliviousness of patients who are congenitally insensitive to pain, or the indifference to pain of leprosy patients. From the more general behavioral point of view, the role of the restorative system (repair and recovery) is associated with negative bodily reactions, that is, reduced movement and manipulation. In other words, the system is constantly on alert and reliably and efficiently deters the organism from impermissible actions during the healing process.

Now that we have a fuller picture of the major ways in which pain performs its basic protective functions, we should better appreciate and respect the precious gift of which Miss C. and Brand's leprosy patients were unfortunately deprived. However, people may not only be deprived, genetically or by disease, of that precious gift of the ability to feel pain; they may also become overwhelmed by it to such a degree that the whole mechanism of pain becomes maladaptive and, instead of signaling threat or danger, starts to threaten, endanger, or even terrorize the unfortunate patients. This can happen when, owing to brain lesions or dysfunctions of the nervous system, pain becomes chronic, often intractable, and, consequently, no longer serves as a warning system or as a symptom of disease. At this point, it becomes a *pain syndrome*, which requires medical attention in its own right. This neuropathic pain (peripheral and central), often followed by hyperpathia (allo-dynia, hyperesthesia, hyperalgesia), is more a curse or menace than *poena,* the biological punishment for behavior that may lead to injury or worsen an already inflicted injury. Normal pain, like any reasonable punishment, teaches or reminds the subject that some objects and situations should be avoided, and some actions strongly resisted. The psychological and behav-ioral profile of patients suffering from chronic, often intractable, pain is well described by Mitchell in the following way:

Perhaps few persons who are not physicians can realize the influence which long-continued and unendurable pain may have on both body and mind. . . . Under such torments the temper changes, the most amiable grow irritable, the bravest soldier becomes coward, and the strongest man is scarcely less nervous than the most hysterical. . . . Nothing can better illustrate the extent to which these statements may be true than the case of burning pain, or, as I prefer to term it, causal-gia, the most terrible of all tortures which a nerve wound may inflict. (Mitchell 1872, p. 196)

And it is true that one of the most dreadful and terrifying exam-ples of the pain system going awry is the case of causalgia, or burning pain:

Causalgia typically appears after a high velocity wound (a bullet, shrap-nel or knife injury) has damaged a major nerve in a limb. Most patients experience surface pain of a burning quality immediately in the periph-ery of the injured extremity, and they develop shiny skin and edema in the affected area. The pain worsens and evolves into constant hyperes-thesia and allodynia (everything touching the area causes pain). With time, the pain spreads and eventually involves the whole limb. Temperature changes, light touch, friction from clothing, blowing air, movement of the limb, and any stimulus that affects the patient's emotional state can exacerbate the pain. Minor events like a cry of a child, the rattling of a newspaper, or watching a television program can provoke intense pain. Consequently, patients suffer greatly, becoming reclusive, withdrawn, and tragically incapacitated by the pain. (Chapman, Nakamura, and Flores 2000, p. 28)

One of the most amazing things about causalgia is that the intolerable, burning pain, which spreads all over the affected limb, is evoked and strengthened by completely innocuous and highly nonstandard stimuli. Imagine excruciating pain being produced by the touch of a feather, puffs of air, or the scenes on your television set. Under these circumstances, the gift of pain is stripped of any biological meaning, for it no longer serves any obvious biological purpose. It is, as Mitchell has observed, just a terrible torture for those who are unfortunate enough to suffer from it.

There are other astonishing examples where pain becomes a highly inadequate, hyperprotective response, which arises only under completely nonstandard stimulus conditions. I am inclined, for reasons that will later become more clear, to call this syndrome *threat hypersymbolia.* This syndrome was discovered and studied by Hoogenraad, who first observed it in a patient with an extensive lesion of the right parietal cortex:

The patient was transferred to an institution for rehabilitation; he was reassessed after eight months. With eyes closed he had loss of superficial sensation (pain and touch) in the left side of his body, more severely in the arm than in the leg, trunk, and face, the distal parts of the extremities being affected most. No delayed pain reaction occurred. . . . Vibration was not perceived. There was lack of awareness of the left half of his body and inability to move his left hand and fingers without visual control. With his eyes open and his gaze directed at his left hand, the patient was able to open and close the hand very slowly. There were no sensory abnormalities on the right side of his body. On seeing that the left part of his body was approached for sensory testing, the patient invariably made a brisk withdrawal movement; at the same time he felt a burning pain that was accompanied by grimacing. On moving about, an incidental contact that was not anticipated did not result in pain and withdrawal. When the patient himself approached his left arm with his right hand there was neither pain nor withdrawal. (Hoogenraad, Ramos, and van Gijn 1994, p. 851)

The peculiar or mysterious aspect of this patient's pain and his brisk withdrawal reactions is the fact that both the pain (accompanied by grimacing), and the withdrawal of his arm as if it had been stung, were evoked exclusively by visual stimuli. Both occurred only when the patient saw someone approach his arm. Mysteriously, the pain and withdrawal were evoked *exclusively* by visual stimuli: namely, when he saw the arm being approached by someone else. As the authors of the study have remarked, a major difference from classical anesthesia dolorosa—pain in an area or region which is numb—"was that the painful reactions in the patient did not occur spontaneously" (ibid.).

How, then, are we supposed to understand these bizarre pain reactions? Upon reflection, we can probably identify with the patient's reflexive withdrawal reaction upon seeing the examiner's instrument approaching his arm. Often, during sensory testing or injection, we initially withdraw the arm briskly upon seeing the examiner's needle or the nurse's syringe approaching it. Sometimes we are actually reproached by the examiner or the nurse for reacting improperly to their approach: "I have not even touched you, let alone hurt you!" But we know the trick; we are well aware that it will hurt, once we are really pricked by the pin or syringe. The sight of the sharp object approaching the arm has been correctly assessed as a threatening visual stimulus, and the arm is consequently spontaneously withdrawn. Of course, on the next trial, we usually try to control this reaction for our own good. More to the point, if repeated approaches of the needle or syringe were *not* followed by the expected pain, these observations would gradually convince us that the sight of the needle no longer represented a threat. So, the next visual presentation of these objects in the vicinity of the arm would not evoke avoidance behavior. As we are soon to learn, in these repeatedly unfulfilled expectations, the specialized threat-detection neurons in the sensory association area of our posterior and parietal cortexes would actually become "convinced" that the visually presented object no longer presented a threat or danger and, thus, need not be avoided. They would evince that "conviction" or "assurance" by dramatically decreasing their mean discharge rates in response to such visual stimuli, eventually becoming completely unresponsive. But the threat hypersymbolia patient's neurons specialized for the detection of novel or threatening visual stimuli obviously never had a chance to reach that "conviction" or "assurance." They were not able to learn to discriminate between real and merely apparent threats, so that during sensory testing, the patient invariably made a brisk withdrawal movement whenever his left arm was approached by the examiner's instrument.

His arm . . . gave him a lot of trouble . . . [for] when he saw the arm being approached by someone it would suddenly move sideways as if it had been stung. The involuntary withdrawal movements of his left arm were so embarrassing that he tied it to his belt. (Hoogenraad, Ramos, and van Gijn 1994, p. 851)

The only exceptions to these embarrassing, uncontrollable, withdrawal movements occurred when the patient himself approached his left arm with his right hand. In that case, he experienced neither pain nor withdrawal. The absence of withdrawal on such occasions is something that we can easily understand by considering our own experience. We know from our own experience that the withdrawal movement on visual threat will not occur if we suddenly approach our left arm with our own right hand (although the avoidance reaction would have been be evoked if somebody else had suddenly approached). In other words, we realize that we cannot sneak up on ourselves. The invariable, persistent withdrawal of the patient's arm, whenever it was approached by someone else, remains a mystery. Even more mysterious is the regular appearance of burning pain evoked solely by visual stimuli. To demystify these highly bizarre phenomena we have to examine in more detail the evidence that tells us that there exist, in the sensory association area of the posterior parietal cortex, specialized multisensory neurons whose role is to integrate somatosensory nociceptive inputs and visual inputs in order to provide "an overall sense of intrusion and threat to the physical body and self" (Price 2000, p. 1771).

This evidence comes from electrophysiological, behavioral, and lesion studies in monkeys and humans. The first discovery was the existence of neurons, in area 7b of the monkey brain, that were sensitive to, or responded preferentially to, noxious stimuli. Among these nociceptive neurons, a subpopulation of neurons was found that reliably encoded both harmful thermal stimuli and the degree of their harmfulness. These neurons started to respond to thermal stimulus intensities around 47°C and monotonically increased their mean discharge rates over temperature shifts from 47° to 51°C: that is, the temperature at which nerves start to be damaged, or would be damaged if the stimulus was not discontinued (Dong et al. 1994).

Complementary behavioral studies in monkeys have shown that the stimulus intensity-response functions of these nociceptive cells closely approximate their stimulus intensity-escape frequency function. In other words, thermal stimulus intensities sufficient to evoke an escape response in more than 50 percent of the monkeys were exactly those to which thermal nociceptive neurons best or most reliably responded (ibid.). This makes them perfectly and distinctively suitable to play the role of neurons that alert an organism to the presence of threatening thermal stimuli, and evoke avoidance or escape responses. It turns out that these neurons are actually multisensory—they respond to both thermal and *visual* threats. The visual stimuli to which they best responded were the approach of novel or threatening objects; and their mean discharge rate was *decreased* by repeated presentation of the same novel or threatening object. However, their increased discharge would resume in response to a repeatedly presented object after it was again used to apply a painful stimulus (Robinson and Burton 1980). So it seems that these multisensory neurons are capable of learning and relearning the threatening significance of visual stimuli, and of giving assurances and reassurances with regard to the potentially dangerous character of such stimuli. This brings to mind Wittgenstein's famous remark about the situations that disclose the true nature and causes of certainty:

The character of the belief in the uniformity of nature can perhaps be seen most clearly in the case in which we fear what we expect. Nothing could induce me to put my hand into a flame, although after all it is only in the past that I have burnt myself. (Wittgenstein 1968, §472)

I shall get burned if I put my hand in the fire: that is certainty.

That is to say: here we see the meaning of certainty. (What it amounts to, not just the meaning of the word "certainty.") (Ibid., §474)

One could say that, when we are watching our hand closely approaching the fire, our certainty that we shall get burned if we put our hand in the fire is the certainty bestowed upon us by the "certainty" that our multisensory nociceptive neurons have reached by firing vigorously at the visual presentation of the hand approaching the fire. Notice that the possibility of giving a neurological explanation of one of our basic epistemic categories—that of certainty—is at stake. This is the only way, as far as I can see, in which one can give sense and substance to the venerable project of naturalizing epistemology. This project is well underway in cognitive neuroscience, where it falls under the more modest and more precise heading: "What can the brain tell us about the mind?" In this context, and related to the topic of the neurological grounds of basic forms of certainty, one should also mention that, quite recently, pertinent electrophysiological studies in conscious humans have disclosed that there exist neurons in the anterior cingulate cortex that respond selectively to painful mechanical and thermal stimuli. Some of these neurons also respond, like the ones discovered in monkeys, to threatening or potentially dangerous visual stimuli:

Interestingly, this cell also responded when the patient watched pin-pricks being applied to the examiner's fingers. When pinpricks were again applied to the patient, the response started before skin was contacted, suggesting a response to pain anticipation. (Hutchison et al. 1999, p. 404)

Let us, after this necessary digression, return to the consideration of one more important property of nociceptive multisensory neurons. Namely, one should also take into account the significant fact that they will respond or, upon repeated presentations, cease to respond, to visual stimuli, *only* if these stimuli are located near the arm or face. That is, their receptive

fields are not retinotopically but rather somatotopically organized, and are congruent with cutaneous receptive fields of nociceptive neurons on the arm. This is why they best, or only,
respond to visual stimuli approaching the seen hand at the distance of 10 to 20 centimeters, or directed at that distance toward
the face. As a consequence of the visuo-nociceptive integration,
the activation of the multisensory neurons by a visual stimulus
closely approaching the left arm will also activate the corresponding somaesthetic representation of that arm and enhance
the activity of thermal nociceptive neurons. If that is the case,
it does not seem improbable that seeing could produce feeling.

Lesion studies and clinical observation have shown that
damage to the posterior parietal cortex often results in weakness
or paralysis affecting the contralesional upper limb, and complete somatosensory loss in that limb. That is, patients are
unable to move the arm opposite the lesion or feel sensations
in any modality. Neurological somatosensory assessment is
usually carried out with the patient's eyes closed. However, in
one study conducted on a large sample of patients suffering
from somatosensory loss in the contralesional arm, the assessment was done with the patients' eyes open. Patients were
instructed to look at their affected arm when it was touched by
the experimenter. No patient couid feel any sensations with his
or her eyes closed, but two patients reported having felt the
experimenter's touch when they were allowed to see the arm
being stimulated (Halligan et al. 1997). In one patient, seeing
an on-screen image of the affected hand being touched produced reports of tactile sensation in the affected hand, even if
no real touch occurred.

Hoogenraad's threat hypersymbolia patient could not feel any
sensation (pain or touch) in his left arm when he kept his eyes

closed during the sensory testing, nor could he move his left hand or his fingers during motor testing. However, with his eyes open and his gaze directed toward his left hand, he was able to open and close the hand very slowly. Vision was of great help in enabling and facilitating the desperately needed motor movements of the left hand. But vision was also the source of great embarrassment and undeserved suffering as far as his left arm was concerned: the mere sight of his left arm being approached by the examiner's instrument evoked involuntary withdrawal and the feeling of burning pain accompanied by grimacing. So here we have another case of a visual event producing feeling in an otherwise anesthetic limb, although in this case, seeing evoked the more spectacular feeling of burning pain. But the case that we are interested is much more than just another example of seeing producing feeling. It is actually a case in which the human pain protective system has gone irreparably awry, causing permanent misery to the unfortunate sufferer. The neural basis of this damage is a vicious circle that occurs when brain damage prevents the neuronal dissociation or uncoupling that would normally lead to relearning. This neuronal vicious circle put a spell of threat on Hoogenraad's unfortunate patient. He was no longer able to discriminate between visual stimuli that were threatening and those that were not. Every visual stimulus approaching his hand would, under any conditions, be assessed by him as a potentially dangerous stimulus. That is why we can describe his as a case of threat hypersymbolia.

But how did the neuronal vicious circle responsible for this highly maladaptive and bizarre behavior get established? Well, owing to the damage of the right posterior parietal lobe, the nociceptive neurons of the sensory association area could not receive any more somatosensory inputs associated with the noxious mechanical or thermal stimulation of the left arm. However, because these neurons are multisensory, they can also be triggered by specific kinds of visual stimuli. As we have seen, these nociceptive multisensory neurons respond best to novel or threatening visual objects, which the subject must see approaching his arm. When such stimulus is presented—for instance, when the examiner's instrument approaches the left arm—multisensory nociceptive neurons will respond. When these neurons are activated, visual integration will activate the corresponding somaesthetic representation of the arm. This will, in turn, stimulate thermal nociceptive neurons to project the sensation of burning pain to the left arm, and induce brisk removal of the arm from the path of the approaching object. During sensory testing with eyes opened and the patient's gaze directed at the left arm, each new visual presentation of the object gives rise to burning pain in the arm. Therefore, there is no way in which that the threatening significance can be detached or uncoupled from the sight of the instrument approaching the patient's left arm. To put this point into neural terms, there is no way in which patient's multisensory neurons responding to visual stimuli can be "reassured" and decrease their mean discharge rate upon the next visual presentation of the instrument, or cease to respond to it. In this way the vicious circle is established: the visual stimulus giving rise to burning pain and the regular appearance of this pain upon visual stimulation reinforces the threatening meaning of the visual stimulus, so that it always recruits the multisensory neurons that distinctively respond to visual objects closely approaching the subject's hand.

How vicious that circle is may best be appreciated if we consider how we might help the patient to get out of it. The first

strategy that comes to mind is, of course, the strategy of relearning, or retraining the neural mechanism that has gone astray
which is responsible for the patient's uncontrollable overreac-
tions to visual stimuli. One strategy would be to repeatedly
present the visual object in such a way that its presentation
would not be followed by the feeling of burning pain in the
arm. Thus, the multisensory neurons situated in the sensory
association area of the right posterior parietal lobe would no
longer respond to the relevant visual stimulus and the corresponding feeling of burning pain would no longer be evoked by
their activity. In short, seeing would no longer produce feeling
in the otherwise anesthetic left arm. But this strategy is doomed
to failure because, in this patient, every visual presentation of
the instrument approaching his left arm invariably produces the
feeling of burning pain in that arm.

We could also try to hold the arm firmly while the patient
watched the instrument approaching his left arm, and try
to induce the innocuous tactile sensation by the instrument,
hoping that the corresponding visual information might "boost
sub-threshold tactile stimulation into conscious awareness"
(Halligan et al. 1997, p. 203). This neural retraining strategy
would basically be an attempt to couple the innocuous character of the tactile sensation to the sight of the instrument. The
repetition of this sequence could lead to the reassessment of the
visually presented object as a mock threat. That is, it might
eventually "reassure" the multisensory neurons and decrease or
eliminate their response to such stimuli. The problem with this
strategy, which is so salutary and effective in ordinary cases, is
that it just wouldn't work for the patient that we are interested
in. Again, for him, each visual presentation of the approaching
instrument would cause the feeling of burning pain, and this

feeling would inhibit the appearance of any other concurrent sensations, particularly innocuous ones. As Sherrington observed, pain can suppress or override all other concurrent sensations. This means that tactile sensations evoked by innocuous stimulation could not be felt, and therefore that their innocuousness would not be associated with the antecedent or concurrent visual stimulus:

It would seem a general rule that reflexes arising in species of receptors which considered as sense organs provoke strongly affective sensations ceteris paribus prevail over reflexes of other species when in competition with them for the use of the "final common path." Such reflexes override and set aside with peculiar facility reflexes belonging to touch organs, muscular sense organs, etc. As the sensations evoked by these arcs, e.g. "pains," exclude and dominate concurrent sensations, so do the reflexes of these arcs prevail in the competition for possession of the common paths. They seem capable of pre-eminent intensity of action. (Sherrington 1948, p. 232)

What holds for dominant reflexes is obviously also valid for dominant sensations: pains are certainly capable of *preeminent intensity* of feeling and, consequently, of action. This is another reason why there is no way out of the vicious circle into which the patient's protective pain mechanism has fallen—at least not via relearning or retraining. This now vicious "self-protective" system is completely encapsulated and totally impenetrable to any functional reorganization. It operates from its own internally justified premises. This broken system has an internal logic, which holds unless it is considered from a perspective external to the mechanisms to which it is applied. As Descartes observed, this perspective is a kind of external denomination with regard to the mechanisms:

A clock composed of wheels and counter-weights no less exactly observes the laws of nature when it is badly made, and does not show the time properly, than when it entirely satisfies the wishes of its maker. . . . And although considering the use to which the clock has been destined by its maker, I may say that it deflects from the order of its nature when it does not indicate the hours correctly . . . , nevertheless I recognize at the same time that this last mode of explaining nature is very different from the other. For this is but a purely verbal characterization depending entirely on my thought, which compares . . . a badly constructed clock with the idea which I have of a . . . well made clock, and is hence extrinsic to the things to which it is applied. (Descartes 1968, p. 195)

Descartes's badly made clock observes the laws of nature exactly, even though it does not show the correct time. Analogously, the patient's badly made or damaged protective pain mechanism strictly adheres to basic neural and behavioral principles, although it does not show the threat properly and does not evoke the feeling of pain properly. From the internal point of view, the mechanism is put into action like any other normal mechanism: nociceptive multisensory neurons specialized for the detection of novel or potentially threatening visual objects start to fire when the instrument is seen approaching the arm. As the visual presentation of the approaching instrument evokes the feeling of burning pain, the dangerous character of the visual stimulus is confirmed, and the specialized nociceptive multisensory neurons will fire more vigorously on the next presentation of the visual stimulus. There is nothing that can decrease or inhibit their firing. But nor would there be anything to decrease or inhibit the firing of these specialized neurons under normal circumstances, that is, when repetitive visual presentations of the needle closely approaching one's arm would invariably be followed by the pain inflicted by that needle. It is not improbable that, after such "visuo-doloric" training, the "normal" protective pain system would start to produce pain simply at the sight of the arm being approached by the needle. But the "normal" system could, luckily, be retrained, whereas the patient's vicious system would resist any retraining. The patient discovered his own solution to avoid the highly embarrassing involuntary withdrawal of his left arm whenever he saw someone approaching it; his solution was to tie his left arm to his belt. But the other part of the problem remained even after eight months of rehabilitation: the burning pain and suffering that would appear as a punishment whenever he saw someone approaching his left arm. The fact that seeing can produce the feeling of pain is no longer completely mysterious to us. We have enough insight into the neural mechanism of pain to allow us to explain, or come close to explaining, how that extraordinary phenomenon is possible. But there is one problem related to that knowledge. Ideally, knowledge is supposed to give us power or control over nature, but in the case of the vicious circle that we have been considering, it actually explains why we are powerless or helpless with regard to such pain, and why the pain that the unfortunate patient is suffering cannot be controlled. We can solve, and are close to solving, the theoretical or intellectual puzzle of that vicious pain. Despite our theoretical sophistication, we still do not know how to cure it, or even whether a cure is possible. Until that puzzle is solved, our knowledge of pain mechanisms will seem modest compared to the amount of suffering that it still cannot relieve.

3 Dissociation Phenomena in Human Pain Experience

As far as the possible biological and psychological dysfunctions or disruptions of the human pain protective system are concerned, we have until now considered only the most extreme or dramatic cases of such dysfunctions or disruptions: the total absence of pain and the complete maladaptive excessiveness and inadequacy of pain. But more often people are only partially deprived of the gift of pain. They can lose, owing to lesions, or surgical, pharmacological, or cognitive manipulations, irreversibly or temporarily, just a portion of that gift. This observation will lead us to the consideration of the dissociation syndromes of human pain experience. One example of such dissociations is the complete loss, fortunately reversible, of the capacity to display any behavioral reactions upon long-lasting, intensive, painful stimulation, even though the pain is felt in all its severity, is of excruciating character, and is totally unbearable. Patients who were unfortunate enough to undergo major surgeries under the influence of curare experienced this radical dissociation of the behavioral aspect of pain from its affective and sensory components: the complete absence of the former and the full presence of the latter. In the 1940s, however, many physicians believed that curare was an effective general anesthetic:

The patients were, of course, quiet under the knife, and made not the slightest frown, twitch or moan, but when the effects of the curare wore off, complained bitterly of having been completely conscious and in excruciating pain, feeling every scalpel stroke but simply paralyzed and unable to convey their distress. The doctors did not believe them. Eventually a doctor bravely submitted to the elaborate and ingenious test under curare, and his detailed confirmation of the subject's reports was believed by his colleagues: curare is definitely not any sort of anesthetic or analgesic. (Dennett 1978, p. 433)

It turned out that curare is not an anesthetic at all; it is a paralytic which "acts directly on all the neuromuscular junctions, the last rank effectors of the nervous system, to produce total paralysis and limpness of all the voluntary muscles" (ibid., p. 432). This is why curarized patients could not express their distress and agony, make any verbal complaints, display any avoidance or escape reactions, moan, or make grimaces while experiencing excruciating pain. To the great relief of behaviorists, it should be remarked that the case of curarized patients cannot be taken as conclusive evidence that one can be in pain without even having the slightest tendency, inclination, or disposition toward any form of pain behavior. As we have seen, there is, indeed, in these patients a very prominent inclination, tendency, or disposition to express their pain and to react to it; but, owing to muscular paralysis, they lack any means to realize that inclination, tendency, or disposition; they are unable to translate it into verbal expression or into any bodily actions or reactions.

So, the question is whether one can one feel pain, in the strict sense of the term, and yet not have even the slightest tendency or disposition toward pain behavior. In other words, can one be completely indifferent to pain? But complete indifference to pain would also mean that one is not at all distressed by pain; that pain is no longer the object of anxiety, fear, or dread; that pain does not signify threat or danger; and, finally, what is hardest to understand, that pain is no longer disliked or experienced as inherently unpleasant. Such indifference to pain would actually mean that the emotional-cognitive and behavioral components of pain experience would be dissociated from its sensory-discriminative components: that one would be able to feel pain, localize it, determine its intensity and qualitative character, and yet not react to it in any way. If that is possible, it would be a case of a radical reactive dissociation syndrome in human pain experience. The postoperative condition of patients who have undergone prefrontal lobotomies to treat chronic pain is often regarded as the paradigm case of an extreme reactive dissociation syndrome—or at least of striking indifference to pain. After the operation, these patients typically report that their pain is still present, but that it doesn't does not bother them anymore, and/or that they do not mind or care about it anymore. Here, the behavioral patterns and emotional-cognitive profile of one lobotomized patient are depicted by Paul Brand:

I have had limited contact with lobotomized patients, but while in India I did see in one patient dramatic evidence of lobotomy's effect on pain. British woman from Bombay had for years sought relief from intractable vaginal pain. She tried every available pain-relieving pill, and even underwent surgery to sever nerves, but nothing helped.

A neurosurgeon on our staff had perfected a technique for lobotomy. . . . He would drill holes on both sides of the skull, run a wire through them, and then . . . use the wire to slice through nerve pathways and separate the frontal lobes from the rest of the brain. He explained the risks to the woman, who immediately agreed to the surgery. She was ready to try anything.

By all measures, the lobotomy was a great success. The woman emerged from surgery completely free of the suffering that had shadowed her for a decade.

More than a year later I visited (her) in Bombay. . . . When I inquired about the pain, she said, "Oh, yes, it's still there. I just don't worry about it anymore." She smiled sweetly and chuckled to herself. "In fact, it's still agonizing. But I don't mind."

At the time it startled me to hear words about agony coming from a person with such a placid demeanor: no grimace, no groan, only a gentle smile. As I read about other lobotomies, however, I found she was displaying a very typical attitude. Patients report feeling "the little pain without the big pain." A lobotomized brain, no longer recognizing pain as a dominating priority in life, does not call for a strong aversive reaction. (Brand and Yancey 1997, pp. 210–211)

A similar behavioral pattern and emotional-cognitive profile is found in the patients who have undergone cingulotomy, another type of psychosurgery for chronic pain. It was assumed that the cingulate cortex or cingulum, and particularly the anterior cingulate cortex, plays an important role in the affective-cognitive processing of pain:

Therefore, it was attractive to postulate that transection of the cingulum might be of benefit in those clinical cases of intractable pain in which marked emotional factors appeared to contribute to the intolerable situation.

In this project [the] intent was to modify the patient's emotional response to the life-threatening situation which he faced so that his expression of fear and anxiety no longer augmented critically whatever pattern of organic pain was present to produce intolerable suffering. (Foltz and White 1962, p. 89)

The immediate effects of cingulotomy on patients' affective and cognitive attitudes toward pain are described in the following way:

Immediate results from the lesions usually were apparent in the operating room. Continued verbal communication was maintained with each patient during the operation in order to evaluate to some degree his emotional state and degree of pain. A complaining, uncomfortable, apprehensive patient usually showed a dramatic change in demeanor at the time the lesions were made. The patient became tractable, agreeable and often showed a little vague disorientation. In two instances, this change occurred concomitant with simple insertion of the electrodes into the area of the cingulum prior to electro-coagulation. (Ibid., p. 92)

The long-lasting effects of this invasive psychosurgical procedure on patients' affective and cognitive attitudes toward ongoing, chronic pain are vividly illustrated by the following case study of a typical cingulotomy patient:

Case I-3. M.W., 68-year-old white female, had been suffering from intense burning vaginal and perineal pain for over 2 years. . . . The Department of Psychiatry felt she had "severe depression with maximum anxiety." The Department of Neurosurgery decided on cingulotomy because of the complaints of severe, incapacitating pain associated with complex emotional factors.

After cingulotomy, the change was indeed striking. She ceased her continual whining complaints, began to take note of her external environment, and began to move about again. Within two weeks, she was up and walking for the first time in nine months. Shortly, she was able to leave the hospital, returned home, and resumed her housework activities. On questioning her, the pain was still present but did not concern her now. Over a four-year follow-up, her complaints of pain have not returned to clinical significance. (Ibid., pp. 93–94)

Morphine is said to have similar effects on pain perception to those observed in lobotomized and cingulotomized patients. Under the influence of morphine subjects also claim that their pain is still there, and that it continues to be *pain*, but that they no longer mind it. Because of this carefree attitude toward pain, or carefree feeling of pain, some researchers "describe the action of morphine (and some barbiturates) as reversible pharmacological leucotomy (lobotomy)" (Dennett 1978, p. 430).

We have reviewed the three cases that are usually cited as typical cases of indifference to pain, or outstanding examples of radical reactive pain dissociation syndromes. However, the indifference toward pain displayed in lobotomized and cingulotomized patients, and patients under the influence of morphine, is of limited scope. Moreover, this indifference is not necessarily directed toward the very sensation of pain, or the immediate threat that it imposes to the patient. Often this indifference stems from the significance with which the patient attaches to the pain. Indifference to pain or a carefree attitude toward it need not mean that the pain is not felt as unpleasant. Let me describe one situation that speaks strongly in favor of the last two claims about the kind of indifference toward pain displayed by lobotomized, cingulotomized, and morphinized patients. This situation might well be familiar to you from your own experience: Imagine that you have a prolonged dull, nagging pain in your upper left chest radiating down your left arm. This pain is not only unpleasant, annoying, and distressing in the short run—it may also evoke strong anxiety and fear because it can be taken as a sign of an impending heart attack. If your physician reassures you and explains that the real cause of the pain is muscular inflammation, the anxiety and fear will subside. You will take a carefree attitude toward the pain, although the pain will still be there and will still be felt as unpleasant. As far as the scope of indifference toward pain is concerned, it should be said that in lobotomized, cingulotomized, and morphinized patients, their carefree attitude is strictly limited to the ongoing pain in question. They will vigorously react to new pain provoked by sudden, intense stimuli.

So, once again, the question is: can one be completely indifferent toward pain in the sense of not minding at all for any pain inflicted by harmful stimulation and not having the slightest tendency or disposition toward any form of pain behavior?

In other words, can one regularly feel pain upon harmful stimulation, localize it, and assess its intensity and qualitative character, and yet never dislike it, be distressed by it, fear it, worry about it, or try to avoid it? Is such pain without any painfulness possible? Can we even imagine such a possibility? Are we at least able to conceive of it—or is it something that surpasses our imagination and is to be proclaimed impossible on grounds of inconceivability?

In order to give an answer to these perplexing questions, I will invite the reader to imagine the following scenario. Try to imagine a person who, during thorough daily neurological sensory discrimination tests, feels pain and recognizes its quality, intensity, and location whenever severe harmful stimuli are applied to any part of his body, but never finds it in the least unpleasant and never does anything about it. He shows no withdrawal whatsoever, no grimacing, no wincing, no complaints, nor even the slightest tendency toward these common reactions to pain. Imagine further that this person, upon being challenged by his astonished neurologist to explicitly state whether he feels the corresponding harmful stimuli, says that he, indeed, feels them; that they hurt him a bit, but that they do not bother him and mean nothing to him. Moreover, and to the even greater astonishment of the examiner, this imagined patient laughs or smiles while being exposed to obviously harmful or even torturing stimuli, and he abruptly stops making fun of the pain when the stimuli are discontinued. And to the utter surprise and relief of the neurologist, the patient maintains his friendly demeanor, never becoming angry or annoyed at the doctor— even though such a neurologist would normally (and justifiably) be regarded as more of a torturer than an examiner. Add to this that our imagined patient never displays any avoidance or protective reactions when approached by the examiner's tools, such as needles or hot probes, nor does he show any signs of anticipatory anxiety. On the contrary, sometimes he even willingly offers his hands for painful testing. The same absence of any motor and affective reactions is observed in him in response to visual threats or verbal menaces: no flinch, no blink, and no expression of fear. The imaginary person is to be conceived as being quite unaware of his plight, and of the fact that his reactions to pain are highly abnormal. He is also supposed to be unable to learn appropriate escape or avoidance reactions, despite the fact that he feels pain whenever a harmful stimulus is inflicted upon him. Finally, imagine what terrible things might happen to this person in the real world. There is no doubt that the integrity of his body would be constantly threatened. For example, he could easily suffer serious burns without any escape or affective reactions.

One might claim that this imaginary case of pain without any painfulness, of pure pain reduced to totally indifferent sensory detection and discrimination of injurious stimuli, is not something that could ever really be found in human pain experience, but is rather something that will at best remain, to use Eliot's phrase, a perpetual possibility only in the world of speculation. Given our everyday experience of pain, this judgment may well seem to us to be the only proper one to make as far as the possibility of ever disclosing such pain in humankind is concerned. As Patrick Wall, one of the most distinguished figures in the field of pain research and theory, put it: "I have never felt a pure pain. Pain for me arrives as a complete package. A particular pain is at the same time painful, miserable, disturbing, and so on. I have never heard a patient speak of pain isolated from its companion affect" (Wall 1999, p. 149). An even more apodictic and exclusive statement along the same lines is to be found in Valerie Hardcastle's book, *The Myth of Pain*: "Except under unusual circumstances, we cannot react to pain without also bringing forth a lot of additional baggage. There is no such thing as a simple pain state, nor a simple pain" (Hardcastle 1999, p. 114).

But we know that there is such a thing as pure pain because there is ample evidence that patients with pain asymbolia experience exactly this kind of pain whenever they are harmfully stimulated anywhere on their bodies. Ever since the appearance of Schilder and Stengel's seminal paper entitled *Schmerzasymbolie* (1928, pp. 143–148), there have been clinical reports of patients who feel pain that is literally deprived of any painfulness, who can "recognize pain but lack appropriate motor and emotional responses to painful stimuli applied anywhere on the body surface. They may also appear insensitive to visual threats and to verbal menaces" (Berthier, Starkstein, and Leiguarda 1988, p. 41). In other words, when I initially invited the reader to imagine a person who feels pain without, so to say, being in pain, I was not relying on a fanciful thought experiment devised to probe our deeply entrenched intuitions about human pain experience. Rather, I was basing the example on real-life cases well documented by relevant clinical evidence. The fact that such pain may seem inconceivable is just proof that real life surpasses our imagination, and that conceivability is not always a reliable guide to possibility. That is, the amazing and quite incomprehensible experiential report that our imaginary person was supposed to make when challenged by the astonished neurologist, as well as the smiling that he was meant to display on that occasion, has been actually made and displayed by a patient suffering from pain asymbolia: "*To painful stimuli the patient responded with almost complete absence of protective and escape reactions*. At the same time from her reports it could be gathered that she is sensitive to painful stimulus: 'I feel it indeed; it hurts a bit, but doesn't bother me; that is nothing,' and so on. She smiles while saying this . . ." (Pötzl and Stengel 1937, p. 180).

One might try to dismiss this extraordinary observation as just one more instance of that perplexing indifference to pain already found in lobotomized, morphinized, and cingulo-tomized patients, and epitomized in their astonishingly carefree reports to the effect that something strange or odd is happening: "The pain is still there, but it doesn't bother me." These reports are normally taken as strong evidence that, owing to reactive disassociation obtained by surgical or pharmacological manipulations, pain need not be experienced as unpleasant and that we should, accordingly, give up our deeply entrenched intuition that it is something intrinsically or essentially disagreeable. So, within this conceptual and theoretical framework, the cases of pain asymbolia would mainly be treated as just more of the same: as an additional piece of evidence that the disassociation between sensory and affective aspects of pain is possible and that pain should thus be considered as only causally or contingently related to unpleasantness.

I will try to show that, on the contrary, pain asymbolia is to be regarded as the only clear-cut case in which severe pain is not experienced as unpleasant at all, and in which there are no traces of any other aversive attitude toward it. Moreover, I will present conclusive evidence that, in contrast to the cases of lobotomized, cingulotomized, and morphinized patients, the case of patients suffering from pain asymbolia should be considered as the only case of complete, thoroughgoing indifference to pain. In other words, I will claim that among the sensory-affective disassociation syndromes to be found in human pain experience, pain asymbolia is the sole case in which all affective reactions to pain are literally lost for good, while the sensory aspect of pain is fully preserved. The indifference to pain displayed in the statement "I feel pain, but it doesn't bother me at all," may well vary, from one syndrome to another, with regard to its scope and its proper object. As it will turn out, only in the case of pain asymbolia is this attitude consistently held toward all pain and directed not only to the possible significance or meaning of pain, but also to the very sensation of pain or the immediate threat that it poses to the subject.

Pain asymbolia holds a unique place among reactive dissociation syndromes in yet another respect: namely, it is distinguished by the total absence of any appropriate pain behavior and any tendency or disposition toward such behavior. As such, the case of pain asymbolia is the most convincing evidence that pain without any appropriate pain behavior is possible. In other words, it can be taken as the strongest evidence against the behaviorist claim that at least the tendency toward pain behavior is necessary to the experience of pain, for in asymbolia patients there is not the slightest tendency toward such behavior, although they feel pain when harmful stimuli are applied anywhere on their bodies. Moreover, these patients, when exposed to harmful stimuli and when feeling quite intense pain, often behave in ways that would by any standards be considered just the opposite of typical pain behavior: they smile in response to painful stimuli, welcome them and maintain a friendly attitude toward persons who are injuring them.

One might well acknowledge the uniqueness of pain asymbolia among the reactive disassociation syndromes to be found in human pain experience, but still claim that such freak possibilities, disclosed in clinical and brain studies, should be discounted. One reason for this harsh verdict might be that these possibilities cannot in any way be relevant for our concept of pain or for our understanding of what it is to be in pain. They should be treated just as extreme aberrations, residing far away from the core phenomenon, on its very edges or even going well beyond them. I will reject this verdict as unwarranted and claim that, on the contrary, thorough and careful consideration of the cases of pain asymbolia may well reveal to us the truly complex nature of pain, its major constitutional elements, the proper role they play in overall pain experience, and the way they work together, as well as the basic neural structures and mechanisms that subserve them. More specifically, I will argue that the consideration of these cases gives us the unique opportunity to clearly and fully see how much is missing, and what exactly is missing, in pain experience once it is deprived of all its affective, cognitive, and behavioral components, while its sensory aspect is kept intact. This insight will, in its turn, make us realize that pain, when stripped of the former components, loses all its representational and motivational force. It comes to nothing in the sense that it is no longer a signal of threat or damage for the subject, and doesn't move (*emotio*) his mind and body in any way. If that is the case, it follows that the basic representational and motivational force of pain should not be sought in its sensory components, but rather in its affective, cognitive, and behavioral dimensions.

4 Pain Asymbolia

In the previous chapter, I issued some promissory notes for the far-reaching conceptual and theoretical implications of pain asymbolia. To make good on these promises, I must describe the sensory, psychological, and behavioral profile of the asymbolic patient in more detail. My exposition and elucidation of the cases of pain asymbolia will rely primarily on the extensive and systematic study of this syndrome carried out by Berthier, Starkstein, and Leiguarda (1988, pp. 41–49). I will also draw on other important cases from the literature which lend support to the findings of Berthier and colleagues. Let us begin with the Berthier, Starkstein, and Leiguarda study. For the purpose of precise and conclusive diagnosis, the authors considered patients to have pain asymbolia "only if they were alert and cooperative; had no evidence of dementia, confusion or previous history of psychiatric disorder; had no deficit in pain perception; and had absent or inadequate motor and emotional responses to painful stimuli applied anywhere on the body surface" (1988, p. 42). After thorough neurological, psychophysical, neuropsychological, and neuroradiological examinations, it turned out that six patients with lesions in specific areas of the brain met these stringent diagnostic criteria for pain asymbolia. The neurological examination of these patients consisted of the following tests.

Perception of superficial pain was assessed through pinpricks and thermal stimuli applied in a single, repetitive, or prolonged way to the face, neck, trunk, limbs, and perineal region. Deep pain was tested by heavy pressure to pretibial, sternal, and supraorbital regions; passive hyperextension of the fingers and toes; squeezing of the calf muscles and the Achilles tendons; and pinching of the soft tissue on all four limbs. Motor responses (withdrawal and grimacing), emotional behavior, and automatic reactions to noxious stimuli were examined. Responses to visual threats were also tested by presenting aggressive gestures in each hemispace, such as pretending to slap the face, punch the nose, or prick the eyes with a needle. The degree of response—whether flinch, blink, or emotional reactions—to such menacing stimuli was recorded. In addition, the extent of reaction to verbal menaces was evaluated by announcing the application of a painful stimulus, with phrases such as "I am going to pinch you hard." Following this verbal threat, a noxious stimulus was given and the response assessed (Berthier, Starkstein, and Leiguarda 1988, p. 42).

The experimenters administered psychophysical tests to measure the following variables:

(1) *pain threshold,* defined as the minimal stimulus intensity perceived as painful; (2) *pain tolerance,* defined as the point at which the stimulus was reported to become intolerable; and (3) *pain endurance,* defined as the arithmetical difference between pain tolerance and pain threshold. Left and right arms were independently stimulated. . . . Bursts of 20 impulses/second lasting 2 seconds were delivered through two ring electrodes to the index finger. Stimuli were delivered every 3 seconds, starting at 0 mA and steadily increasing in intensity to 1 milliangstrom increments. Patients were asked to tell when they began to perceive the

stimulus as painful . . . and when the stimulus became intolerable. After preliminary practice, five trials on each hand were performed and the average was calculated. (Ibid.)

Patients also received a battery of neuropsychological tests of memory and intelligence, as well as tests for aphasia. Patients were observed in the clinic in order to identify possible deficits. All patients received CAT scans to determine the size and location of their lesions. Neurological and psychological testing showed conclusively that the ability to recognize pain upon noxious stimulation was fully preserved in all six patients. But all consistently failed to display any affective or motor responses to painful stimuli. The conspicuous absence of such responses was also observed for visual threats and menaces. Instead of displaying pain behavior, the patients actually displayed the opposite. Here is the case report on one of these patients whose story was a template for the aforementioned "imaginary case" of pain without painfulness:

In spite of apparently normal pain perception of superficial and deep pain, the patient showed a total lack of withdrawal response. He tolerated prolonged pinprick or soft-tissue pinching in all four limbs, without adequate grimacing or defensive movements of his limbs. Neither did he show any response after sternal or supraorbital pressure, thus indicating a generalized defect. Such abnormal findings were constantly recorded throughout daily evaluations of pain. On occasion, the patient willingly offered his hands for pain testing and laughed during stimulation. He had no concern about the defect and appeared highly cooperative during pain evaluation. When the patient was asked specific questions concerning his sensory and affective feelings generated by a noxious stimulus, he tended to underrate the intensity of pain and made no adverse comments. In the course of pain testing sessions he seemed unable to learn proper avoidance responses. Verbal and visual threats also failed to produce protective or emotional reactions.

At times, his lack of withdrawal threatened his safety: his wife reported that he has accidentally suffered a serious left hand burn without escape or emotional reactions. (Ibid., pp. 42–43)

The overall picture of pain asymbolia that emerges from this case report is, with some variation, representative of the pain asymbolics studied, leading the authors to offer the following composite description of their six patients:

Although all 6 patients could adequately recognize painful stimuli and distinguish sharp from dull, all of them showed a lack of response to painful stimuli applied over the entire body. Neither superficial nor deep pain stimulation elicited a motor withdrawal, grimacing, or an appropriate emotional response. One patient not only failed to show a withdrawal response but also exhibited a reaction of "approach" to the painful stimuli (i.e., he directed his limb toward the noxious stimuli). Inappropriate emotional responses were common: 4 patients smiled or laughed during the pain testing procedure. This abnormal behavior ceased abruptly on discontinuing stimulation. All patients appeared quite unaware of their abnormal reactions and seemed unable to learn appropriate escape of avoidance responses. None of them became anxious or angry during the pain testing procedure; in fact, while all could recognize pain, none of them reported any unpleasant feeling. Patients showed normal autonomic reactions (tachycardia, hypertension, sweating, mydriasis) during the painful stimulation, but failed to react with a flinch, blink, or adequate emotional responses to threatening gestures presented to both hemispaces. Five patients also failed to react to verbal menaces. (Ibid., p. 43)

Psychophysical measurements of pain threshold, tolerance, and endurance were carried out in three patients, and five healthy control subjects. "The preservation of pain perception through the measurement of pain threshold failed to reveal a significant difference between patients and a group of normal controls. As expected, all three patients showed significantly greater values for pain tolerance and pain endurance. The patients demonstrated a remarkable increased capacity to endure pain and to underrate the disagreeable stimuli characteristic" (ibid., p. 47). Schilder and Stengel reported that when their patient was pricked on her left hand and asked whether it hurt, they received the following reply: " 'It hurts indeed, but I do not know what that really is.' . . . The patient again said it hurts indeed a bit" (Schilder and Stengel 1928, p. 151). A tendency to underestimate the painfulness of noxious stimuli and to minimize complaining was even more pronounced in the patient examined by Pötzl and Stengel: " 'I feel it indeed; it hurts a bit, but it doesn't bother me; that is nothing,' and so on" (Pötzl and Stengel 1937, p. 180).

Schilder and Stengel were struck by another bizarre behavior in their patient, namely, her "approach" to painful stimuli: her willingness to offer limbs for further painful stimulation. Six decades later, Berthier, Starkstein, and Leiguarda noted the same puzzling tendency in one of their asymbolia patients. According to Schilder and Stengel, there was absolutely no doubt that Anna H. felt pain when she was strongly pricked. However, "the patient didn't evaluate the pain properly. This is revealed by the fact that she didn't at all or insufficiently withdraw from the painful stimulus, and that she even willingly offered herself to it" (Schilder and Stengel 1928, p. 154). A tendency toward pain-induced "approach" behavior was also notable in an asymbolic patient studied by Rubins and Friedman: "He would not withdraw his hands or other parts of the body on painful stimulation (pinprick), although he could distinguish sharp from dull. He would even advance his arms for the painful pinprick" (Rubins and Friedman 1948, p. 559). So, it seems that at least some asymbolics not only fail to display normal reactions to painful stimuli, but actually behave in the exact opposite way.

Pain-approaching behavior is relatively rare among pain asymbolics, but another inappropriate and perplexing reaction of pain asymbolics, that of smiling of laughing during painful testing, is much more common. In fact, it seems to be virtually the norm for these patients. Berthier, Starkstein, and Leiguarda report that, in their sample of six patients conclusively diagnosed with pain asymbolia, four smiled or laughed during painful testing, and abruptly stopped acting amused when painful stimulus was withdrawn. This weird and incomprehensible reaction to pain was described in the first clinical observation of pain asymbolia, Schilder and Stengel's study of Anna H. Ms. H displayed the following reaction to a pinprick on the palm of her right hand: "The patient laughs contentedly, jerks the palm lightly, says 'oh hurts, that hurts,' smiles on it, but stretches the hand further toward the examiner and turns on all sides" (Schilder and Stengel 1928, p. 147). The same odd reaction was elicited in Pötzl and Stengel's patient during pain testing (Pötzl and Stengel 1937, p. 180). In a recently published article, Ramachandran describes an asymbolic patient he met in India. Ramachandran reports that the patient "not only failed to experience the aversive quality of the pain but started laughing in response to pinprick!" (Ramachandran 1998, p. 1857). Ramachandran's amazement prompted him to ask the following question: "Is this not the ultimate irony: laughter in response to pain?" (ibid.). But this is neither the sole nor the final irony in the responses of asymbolia patients to painful stimuli. As recorded by Berthier, Starkstein, and Leiguarda, all their patients were highly cooperative and none of them became anxious or angry during testing, even though they were subjected daily to powerful, noxious stimuli. This amazing attitude was long ago observed by Schilder and Stengel in their patient, Anna H.: "She never blamed the experimenter for inflicting pains to her and kept a friendly, obliging attitude towards him even when the painful stimuli were numerous and very strong" (Schilder and Stengel 1928, p. 154). According to these authors, one testing session which consisted of pricking the patient's left hand with a needle, and her declaring that it indeed hurts her a bit, had quite an unexpected ending: "the patient is cheerful, friendly and bids farewell to the examiner by curtsy" (ibid., p. 151). Is this not the final irony: paying courtesy to your torturer?

This astounding behavior may seem less perplexing if one recalls that patients with pain asymbolia are generally unable to learn to avoid or escape pain. The failure of avoidance goes beyond acutely painful stimuli, like stabbing a needle into the finger, or pressing a hot probe into the palm. Asymbolics also fail to recoil spontaneously from threatening stimuli such as aggressive gestures and verbal menaces, nor can they learn to do so. This deficit was characteristic of nearly all the patients in Berthier, Starkstein, and Leiguarda's study, and this phenomenon is observed in numerous other studies of pain asymbolia. Thus, Schilder and Stengel have explicitly pointed out that their patient "doesn't exhibit any appreciation of pain threat, or of any threat whatsoever. Hitherto the inadequate reactions to very strong optical and acoustic stimuli are certainly to be taken into account" (Schilder and Stengel 1928, p. 154). Rubins and Friedman supply additional evidence for this general lack of threat appreciation or evaluation, which was also prominent in their patient: "In addition to the lack of reaction to painful body stimulation, such as slapping her face, punching her nose, pinching her, or even moving a pin toward her eyes, she did not flinch, blink or react emotionally" (Rubins and Friedman 1948, p. 557).

In the same vein, what was abnormal about Hemphill and Stengel's patient suffering from word deafness and pain asymbolia was not only his lack of normal reactions to painful stimuli, but also his lack of all reactions to any threatening stimuli whatsoever. When the patient was threatened with a prick to his hand or neck, "he made no effort to guard himself or to withdraw his head, nor did he show any instinctive combative reaction. Similarly, he appeared to be quite disinterested when a match was struck close to his face or eyes. He showed the same lack of reaction to unexpectedly loud noises or strong flashes of light" (Hemphill and Stengel 1940, p. 256). As is characteristic of pain asymbolics, the patient perceived and recognized the stimulus (as a poke or a lit match), but he failed to appreciate its meaning or affective valence. The patient was unable to see the stimulus as a threat. So, the patient was unmoved by the stimulus, and remained in a state of complete indifference and inaction. This is best illustrated by the following occurrence: The patient was observed proceeding one morning along the main road of the hospital. He made no effort to get out of the way of a lorry behind him in spite of the loud warning of the horn. That he heard the horn and recognized its character is certain, for he admitted as much with considerable heat when he was forbidden, for his own safety, to walk alone on the main road. It was obvious from his action at the time that when he heard the motor horn he did not react as if it were a sound of warning (ibid.).

Like Hemphill and Stengel's patient, one of the patients studied by Berthier, Starkstein, and Leiguarda also suffered from pure word deafness, while another had a conduction aphasia similar to the patient recorded by Pötzl and Stengel. However,

Berthier, Starkstein, and Leiguarda's four other patients did not display severe neuropsychological deficits. Actually, commonly associated neurological and neuropsychological deficits were "unilateral or bilateral cortical sensory loss, rapidly resolving hemiparesis, unilateral neglect, and disorders of the body schema" (Berthier, Starkstein, and Leiguarda 1988, p. 47). All patients, except one, have received thorough monthly reevaluation for at least six months. The pain asymbolia generally "remained unchanged in all five [patients who received follow-up]." By contrast, the five patients showed substantial recovery from other neurological symptoms such as paralysis, sensory impairment, and disorders of the body schema (ibid., p. 46). An interesting and telling piece of evidence is that, during six months of follow-up, only one out of the five patients "was partially concerned about his condition and became fully aware and even astonished by his pathological laughter during painful stimulation" (ibid.). As far as I know, medical literature contains only one other report of an asymbolic patient who became aware of his ailment and his abnormal reactions to painful stimuli, and that is the one examined by Hemphill and Stengel. This patient had no sensory deficit, but "he did not show the normal reactions of withdrawal and defense to painful stimuli, nor to visual stimuli which usually give rise to such reactions, nor did he respond adequately to warnings of danger" (Hemphill and Stengel 1940, p. 257). The authors describe how the patient tried to rationalize this absence of reactions: The patient soon discovered that the examiners were interested in the way he reacted to painful stimuli. He accordingly tried to explain his reactions by such expressions as "I am not a man who cannot stand pain," or "I am used to that because I have worked on the road," or "Laborers are always hurting themselves; we don't take any notice of it." On the other hand, his wife assured them that he had always been susceptible to pain and had reacted violently whenever his children pricked or pinched him during play (ibid., p. 256).

5 How Is Pain without Painfulness Possible?

The cases of patients suffering from pain asymbolia allow us to say, without any contradiction, that one may feel pain without being in pain. Although pure pain or pain without any painfulness may seem inconceivable or incomprehensible, we must concede that it is possible, given that abundant clinical evidence attests to its existence. But, we may still wonder how such outlandish pain—pain that the victim smiles or laughs at—is possible. According to Berthier, Starkstein, and Leiguarda, earlier authors have considered neuropsychological deficits to be crucial factors in the pathogenesis of pain asymbolia. That is, this syndrome "has been variously ascribed to abnormalities of the body-schema, complex perceptual deficits, an altered relationship between body image and the awareness of pain, specific agnostic defects, and behavioral defects dependent on personality" (Berthier, Starkstein, and Leiguarda 1988, p. 41). However, CAT scans of their patients led Berthier, Starkstein, and Leiguarda to question the conventional wisdom about the pathogenesis of pain asymbolia:

Lesion location was the most important factor associated with the development of the syndrome, as the insular cortex was invariably damaged in every patient. In fact, the development of the severe and persistent

AP syndrome in one of our patients, following a discrete ischemic lesion in the posterior insula and parietal operculum, strongly suggests that the involvement of such structures may be sufficient for the production of the syndrome. (Ibid., p. 47)

The fact that precisely these structures were damaged suggests that pain asymbolia is a sensory-limbic disconnection syndrome. In other words, since the somatosensory cortical areas responsible for the detection of sensory features of noxious stimulus are spared in asymbolia patients, they are able to recognize the modality, qualities, intensity, and location of noxious stimuli. However, the damage to the insula and parietal operculum may disrupt the connections between sensory and limbic structures, impairing the subjects' ability to attach appropriate emotional significance to painful stimuli. If so, we would expect these patients to have abnormal emotional responses to pain. This might explain how small, focal lesions could cause the characteristic dissociation between normal pain perception and adequate emotional responses in pain asymbolia. This sensory-limbic disconnection hypothesis was first put forward by Norman Geschwind in his famous article on disconnection syndromes in animals and humans, albeit more on speculative than evidential grounds (Berthier, Starkstein, and Leiguarda 1988). Geschwind explains his model as follows:

Let's assume that a patient develops a lesion not in the secondary sensory area, but in the connection between the secondary association area and the limbic system. It is conceivable that while the patient could still distinguish the qualities of the stimulus, he would have no emotional response to it.

My speculation would be that the connections from the secondary sensory area to the limbic system would go by way of insular cortex. The lesion causing pain asymbolia would in fact spare the secondary sensory area but involve perhaps parietal operculum and insula, cutting of the connections to the limbic system. (Geschwind 1965, p. 270)

The CAT scans of the six patients studied by Berthier, Starkstein, and Leiguarda all showed lesions of the parietal oper- culum and posterior insula, which, the experimenters believe, strongly support Geschwind's sensory-limbic disconnection model.

The authors were able make Geschwind's model more plau- sible and precise by using experimental technology that had not been available in Geschwind's day. They took this new evidence to show that the relevant cortical structures make the crucial link between sensory and limbic areas, so that the damage to the pos- terior insula and parietal operculum could impair the processing of noxious stimuli by disrupting this connection. Berthier, Starkstein, and Leiguarda found the first such evidence in Mesulam and Mufson's demonstration that the posterior insula is reciprocally connected with the following sensory cortices:

Somatosensory—first and second somatosensory areas, areas 5 and 7b; (2) auditory—superior temporal cortex, granular, postauditory and parainsular cortices, first and second auditory areas; (3) visual—medial portion of inferior temporal gyrus, as well as paramotor cortex and high-order association areas on one hand and basomedial and lateral amygdaloid nuclei on the other. (Berthier, Starkstein, and Leiguarda 1988, p. 48)

On the basis of these cortico-limbic interconnections and the role that posterior insula plays in them, Mesulam and Mufson suggested that sensory-limbic (posterior insula-amygdala) inter- action is crucial for the assessment of the affective-motivational content of perceptual experience (Mesulam and Mufson 1985, p. 216). Influenced by this suggestion, Berthier, Starkstein, and Leiguarda came to the following tentative conclusion:

Thus, if this sensory link is disrupted because of damage to the insula or closely connected structures such as area 7b, patients may still be able to identify modality-specific stimuli (somaesthetic, visual or auditory) but may fail to react with appropriate motor responses or emotional tone, since they cannot attribute any significance to painful or menacing stimuli presented in these modalities. Following this interpretation, the behavior observed in most of our patients could be the result of a trimodal sensory-limbic disconnection. (Berthier, Starkstein, and Leiguarda 1988, p. 48)

However, this interpretation leaves many questions that require much more precise and elaborate answers as far as the behavioral pattern typical for pain asymbolia and the possible anatomical substrates of this syndrome are concerned. The first question regards the fact that patients with pain asymbolia fail to respond with appropriate motor and emotional reactions to painful stimuli applied anywhere on their bodies. That is, pain asymbolia is a *bilateral* deficit in the appreciation of painful stimuli. But the neuroradiological tests conducted by Berthier, Starkstein, and Leiguarda showed that four of their patients had lesions of the insular cortex and parietal operculum on the left side, while two had them on the right side. So, how could a unilateral insular or parietal opercular lesion produce a bilateral deficit in the appreciation of painful or threatening stimuli? The second question concerns the exact nature of the behavioral deficit or syndrome that we call pain asymbolia. Is it a sensory-specific behavioral syndrome, as is suggested by the aforementioned interpretation? Or is it rather a more general multimodal behavioral deficit due to the impairment of higher-level mechanisms of pain processing that integrate somatosensory nociceptive stimuli with other sensory modalities and with memory and learning "to provide an overall sense of intrusion and threat to the physical body and self" (Price 2000, p. 1771)? Closely related to this question are two further questions that must be answered if pain asymbolia is to be understood: Why do patients fail to respond not only to somatic noxious stimuli, but also to visual threats? And why are they unable to learn appropriate escape or avoidance responses to threatening stimuli presented in any modality?

In order to answer some of the questions raised above, Berthier, Starkstein, and Leiguarda had to take a closer look at the role of posterior insula and parietal operculum in the processing of noxious stimuli—for these were the brain structures that were conspicuously damaged in their six patients. They turned to electrophysiological studies of these brain structures in monkeys, research conducted by Robinson and Burton.

In this section, I will discuss Robinson and Burton's results, and I will also take into account the much larger set of electrophysiological, neurobehavioral, and lesion data now available on the nociceptive functions of the posterior insula and parietal operculum in monkeys. This body of evidence will be expanded to include the most recent data on the role that these brain structure structures may play in the processing of pain threat in humans.

But let us first consider in more detail the electrophysiological data that Berthier, Starkstein, and Leiguarda initially considered in order to explain certain puzzling anatomical and behavioral facts about pain asymbolia. Electrophysiologists Robinson and Burton studied the effects of noxious stimuli upon neurons in the secondary somatosensory areas of monkeys. Robinson and Burton discovered that few neurons responding to noxious stimuli were found in the secondary somatosensory area, but that both the granular insula and area 7b contained numerous neurons highly sensitive to such stimuli applied to either side of the body:

Area 7b and granular insula were the major regions containing neurons that responded preferentially or exclusively to noxious or diffuse somatic stimuli. Brief noxious mechanical or noxious thermal stimulation affected 7.5% of the total sample from area 7b.... Although the neurons that responded to noxious, thermal, or diffuse stimulation were found throughout area 7b, there were some indications that these neurons were clustered in certain regions, and they were found within the "whole body" representation within area 7b. (Robinson and Burton 1980, pp. 99–100)

Another interesting and important result of Robinson and Burton's research was their discovery of neurons in area 7b that respond to visual stimuli. But even more important was their observation that a subpopulation of these neurons responded specifically to threatening visual stimuli:

Some neurons responded when the animal was shown an undesired, noxious object, such as a pin that has just been used to deliver a slightly painful prick. These responses stopped, following repeated visual presentation of the pin, or after a lapse of 10–15 minutes. However, a response could be elicited by showing the pin if this object was again used to apply a painful stimulus. Visual presentation of neutral objects, such as a tuning fork, or paintbrush, did not elicit responses from these neurons. (Ibid., p. 101)

Robinson and Burton's findings were significant and helpful in three respects to Berthier, Starkstein, and Leiguarda. First, their experiments showed that damage to the granular insula and the parietal operculum can cause radical impairment of pain processing. Many neurons highly sensitive to noxious stimuli were found in precisely these regions, but not in the secondary somatosensory area. Recall that the damage in pain

asymbolia patients was predominantly insular and parietal opercular damage. In light of Robinson and Burton's findings, it
seems plausible that opercular and insular damage is the major
cause of pain asymbolia, rather than damage to the secondary
somatosensory area, as Biemond claimed (1956, pp. 221–231).
Furthermore, the fact that neurons specifically responsive to
threatening visual stimuli were found in the granular insula and
parietal operculum might explain why asymbolia patients with
damage to these areas failed to react to such stimuli. No similar
neurons have been discovered in the secondary somatosensory
cortex, so the somatosensory hypothesis does not explain why
pain asymbolics are unresponsive to threatening visual stimuli.
Finally, the evidence that there are neurons in the granular
insula and parietal operculum that are bilaterally activated
(highly sensitive to noxious stimuli applied to either side of the
body) sheds light on how a unilateral insular or parietal opercular lesion could give rise to bilateral deficit in the appreciation of painful or threatening stimuli.

The work of Dong et al. has corroborated and expanded upon
Robinson and Burton's findings. Dong and colleagues have
amassed electrophysiological evidence of neurons in the cortical area 7b in monkeys that are preferentially responsive to
noxious stimuli, as well as evidence for the existence of neurons
that are highly sensitive to visually threatening stimuli (Dong
et al. 1994, pp. 542–564). In Dong et al.'s sample of 244 neurons
isolated in the trigeminal region of cortical area 7b and studied,
through microelectrode recording, for their responsiveness to
somatosensory and visual stimulation, they found out that
thermal nociceptive neurons

made up approximately nine percent (21 of 244) of the neurons
that had somatosensory response properties. . . . Thermal nociceptive

neurons responded either exclusively to noxious thermal stimuli (high-threshold thermoreceptive, HTT) or differentially to non-noxious and noxious thermal stimuli (wide-range thermoreceptive, WRT). (Ibid., p. 542)

This group of neurons was, in its turn, particularly examined so that their stimulus intensity-response functions could be precisely determined and correlated to the stimulus intensity-escape frequency functions obtained while the monkeys were performing the pain tolerance task. As far as the sensitivity of thermal nociceptive neurons, both of the HTT and WRT kind, to the increases in noxious thermal stimulus intensities is concerned, it has turned out that these neurons can be functionally differentiated "into subpopulations that did encode (EN) and did not encode (NE) the magnitude of noxious thermal stimuli intensities" (ibid.).

This result was measured by applying calibrated thermal stimulation to the faces of monkeys and recording the stimulus intensity-responses of the relevant neurons to assess whether they increased or decreased their mean discharge frequency in response to rising noxious temperatures. Shifts in thermal stimuli intensities were made from an adapting temperature of 38°C to temperatures ranging from 40 to 51°C. All thermal nociceptive neurons that the researchers examined are known to respond reliably to temperatures of 44°C: some of them (HTT) just at that stimulus intensity level and some (WRT) at that level and the levels below it. The intriguing and important question is how this group of neurons would respond to temperatures above 44°C, and particularly to temperature shifts from 47 to 51°C—because nerves begin to sustain heat damage at approximately 48°C. The relevant measurements yielded the following results:

the two subpopulations of thermal nociceptive neurons, WRT-EN and HTT-EN, graded noxious thermal stimulus intensity by increasing their mean discharge frequency in a monotonic manner to increased noxious temperatures. In contrast the mean discharge frequencies of WRT-NE and HTT-NE neurons decreased precipitously at higher noxious plateau temperatures. . . . Therefore these two other subpopulations of thermal nociceptive neurons . . . did not reliably encode the magnitude of noxious thermal intensity by graded discharge rates. (Ibid., p. 548)

Interestingly, the WRT-EN and HTT-EN thermal nociceptive neurons reliably graded by increasing their mean discharge monotonically over temperature shifts between 47 and 51°C. In other words, these neurons are physiologically specialized to effectively encode harmful thermal stimuli and the degree of their harmfulness. This observation may lead us to surmise that, functionally speaking, they are perfectly and uniquely suited to alert an organism to the presence of threatening or potentially threatening thermal stimuli, and to help the creature avoid or escape from them. This is perhaps why Dong et al. carried out behavioral studies on their sample of three monkeys, to see whether there is a significant correlation between the stimulus intensity-escape functions obtained during the performance of an appetitive tolerance–escape task and the stimulus intensity-response functions of the relevant physiologically specialized subgroup of thermal nociceptive neurons of area 7b. The appetitive tolerance-escape paradigm was used for the measurement of thermal pain tolerance because it presented the monkey with a conflict between two reinforcers:

That is, a choice between a positive reward (acquiring protein-fortified fruit sauce or fruit-flavored water) and negative reward (terminating noxious thermal stimulus). Such a model contains a number of desirable features for assessing behaviors evoked by stimulus intensities above pain threshold . . . : (1) it ensures that subjects adopt conservative

biases for aversive responding during the stimulus period and it operates within a stimulus intensity range that activates nociceptors when
the pain tolerance threshold (50% escape responding) is met or
exceeded; (2) it eliminates any avoidance component by allowing the
experimenter to determine the sequence of stimulus intensities; and (3)
it allows comparisons of escape frequency (percent) and latency to stimulus intensities and estimates the growth rate ... of pain magnitude
from tolerance threshold to nearly 100% escape responding. (Ibid.,
p. 543)

The measurements of thermal pain tolerance in the three
monkeys performing appetitive tolerance-escape tasks conclusively showed that there is, indeed, a significant correlation
between "noxious thermal stimulus intensity and the mean
discharge frequency of individual WRT and HTT neurons and
between the same intensity and mean escape frequency
(thermal pain tolerance)" (ibid., p. 549). That is, for the three
monkeys, "the pain tolerance thresholds (50% escape responding) and corresponding 95% confidence intervals were 48.3 ±
3.8°C, 47.2 ± 1.6°C, and 45.1 ± 3.2°C, respectively" (ibid., p.
547). And it is obvious that the thermal stimuli intensities that
evoked 50 percent escape responses in the monkeys closely
resembled the stimulus intensity response functions of the HTT-
EN and WRT-EN neurons in area 7b: the temperature changes
which these neurons graded by increasing their mean discharge
frequency in a monotonic manner were precisely the temperature intensity shifts from 47 to 51°C. For instance, in one
monkey, HTT-EN neurons encoded the temperature intensity
increase to 48°C that evoked over 50 percent of escape
responses, and their peak mean discharge frequency was at the
thermal stimulus intensity of 49°C that evoked almost 90
percent of escape responses. It should also be said that the stimulus intensity-response functions of the HTT-NE and WRT-NE

neurons—that is, of the neurons that did not reliably encode the magnitude of noxious thermal intensity by graded discharge rates—did not significantly approximate stimulus intensity-escape frequency functions.

It is generally acknowledged that, in contrast to the pain perception threshold, the pain tolerance threshold is not closely related to the sensory-discriminative component of pain. Rather, the pain perception threshold is thought to be much more closely linked to pain's evaluative and affective-motivational components. If that is the case, then the fact that the subpopulation of 7b area nociceptive neurons (HTT-EN and WRT-EN) has stimulus intensity-response functions that are closely and significantly correlated to stimulus intensity-escape functions would speak strongly in favor of the assumption that the activity and distinctive stimulus-response properties of this physiologically specialized group of neurons are much more closely related to the evaluation or appreciation of the threatening or potentially threatening nature of the stimulus, of its aversive character or its affective-motivational valence, than to the mere discrimination of the stimulus. To put this assumption into more psychological terms, the firing and distinctive response properties of the relevant group of neurons would be more strongly associated with the conscious appreciation of pain than to the perception of pain. That this might well be the case was further corroborated by Dong et al., in a complementary lesion study of a monkey that had trauma to the posterior parietal cortex. That brain area was damaged during the electrophysiological and behavioral studies described above, and that provided the examiners the unique opportunity to investigate electrophysiological and behavioral consequences of the lesion, and to compare these responses to those that the animal had displayed before the lesion. Actually, the brain trauma in the relevant area was discovered after Dong et al. had noted, over several daily electrophysiological and behavioral recording sessions, "a sharp reduction in the number of cells . . . with resting discharges or with cutaneous receptive fields and . . . a precipitous decrease in escape frequency to noxious thermal shifts" (1996, p. 580). The trauma itself was due to the unilateral focal cerebral compression that was centered over the inferior lobule of the left posterior parietal cortex and parietal operculum and almost eliminated escape behavior to noxious temperatures applied to the skin on the contralateral maxillary face region:

Multiple comparisons of the mean values showed that before brain trauma, escape frequencies associated with noxious temperatures of 47° to 51°C were significantly greater . . . than the escape frequencies associated with temperatures of 43° to 46°C. After brain trauma, escape frequencies for temperatures of 47° to 51°C were significantly reduced . . . from pre-trauma escape frequencies for the same temperatures and were not significantly different then escape frequencies for temperatures of 43° to 46°C. (Dong et al. 1996, p. 583)

For instance, at the critical noxious temperature intensity of 48°C, the monkey's escape responses were below 10 percent, and went even further down to almost completely disappear in response to shifts in thermal stimulus intensity from 48 to 51°C. However, additional tests were designed to examine whether the damage to the relevant brain area would also lead to the impairment of the monkey's sensory-discriminative capacities, or its ability to detect and discriminate noxious thermal stimuli. For these purposes, the monkey was trained to detect the termination of noxious thermal shifts, applied to the contralateral or ipsilateral maxillary region of the face, from the 48°C plateau temperature to 38°C. And it turned out that nearly all downshifts

from 48° to 38°C were detected (button release) within 8s on the contralateral or ipsilateral face. . . . The same result outcome was obtained when successful trial completion required offset detection of non-noxious thermal shifts (42° to 38°C) applied to the contralateral face. (Dong et al. 1996, pp. 583–584)

What these further results showed is that trauma to the posterior parietal cortex and parietal operculum may well leave the sensory-discriminative capacities of the animal completely intact, while causing thorough impairment of motivational and affective behaviors. In other words, these experiments demonstrated that the animal's capacity to detect and discriminate noxious thermal stimuli with regard to their very appearance and quality may be fully preserved, while its ability to appreciate their threatening or potentially threatening nature, their aversive or affective-motivational valence, may be almost entirely eliminated. One should remember that just such selective deficits in pain experience and pain behavior were characteristic of pain asymbolia syndrome. These patients were quite capable of detecting noxious stimuli, discriminating quality, and feeling pain. But, like the monkey studied by Dong et al., they were incapable of appreciating the threatening nature of such stimuli or displaying any avoidance or escape behavior. Compared to control subjects, their pain tolerance threshold was significantly increased and they systematically underestimated the intensity of the injurious stimuli inflicted upon them. What is more, the pain asymbolia patients had lesions or damage in approximately the same areas of the brain as those found in the brain areas of the monkeys studied by Dong et al. These important lesion and behavioral animal studies provide us with additional and independent evidence that damage to the posterior parietal cortex and parietal operculum may, indeed, lead to selective impairments in pain experience and pain behavior. Thus, they speak strongly in favor of the claim made by Berthier, Starkstein, and Leiguarda that lesion location is the most important factor associated with the development of pain asymbolia—that is, that the distinctive disassociation between the sensory-discriminative and affective-motivational components of pain in asymbolia patients may best be explained on neural grounds.

This conclusion is also supported by most subsequent lesion studies in humans, in which the primary aim is to determine the impact of damage involving the parasylvian cerebral cortex on pain perception thresholds and pain tolerance thresholds of patients who have had trauma to this region of the brain. The MRIs of six patients were evaluated in order to determine "to what extent the following cerebral regions were involved in the lesion: anterior insula, posterior insula, retroinsula, and parietal operculum" (Greenspan, Lee, and Lenz 1999, p. 273). The scans revealed that each patient's lesion involved at least two of these regions, which enabled the examiners to compare more precise lesion locations with the results of the measurements of pain perception thresholds and pain tolerance thresholds in these patients. It turned out that patients with elevated pain perception thresholds had lesions restricted to the parietal operculum and the posterior insula, while the parietal operculum was spared in patients who had normal pain thresholds. Of the four patients who took the pain tolerance tests, only two displayed increased tolerance, and theirs were the two whose lesions involved a large part of the insula. Note that the lesion profile of the six pain asymbolia patients studied by Berthier,

Starkstein, and Leiguarda showed the same pattern of brain damage. The authors of the new lesion study hypothesized that pain tolerance is related more to the affective-motivational aspects of pain. They summarized their conclusion thus:

Our results and Berthier's results support the idea that the insula's role in nociceptive information processing is not related to pain threshold. Rather, the insula is more likely to have a role in the more affective and motivational aspects of pain. (Greenspan, Lee, and Lenz 1999, p. 281)

The electrophysiological single-cell recording study of the response properties of nociceptive neurons in area 7b of the monkeys, carried out by Dong et al., may in yet another respect be important for the understanding of the neural grounds of pain asymbolia. In particular, the study contributes to an explanation of the fact that patients suffering from this syndrome fail to respond, not only to somatosensory, but also to visually threatening stimuli, and are, moreover, unable to learn to avoid such stimuli. As the authors of this study remarked, the thermal nociceptive neurons in area 7b had one outstanding and uncommon feature:

A prominent and unusual feature of WRT and HTT neurons in area 7b was their multi-modal properties (responsiveness to both thermal and mechanical stimulation) (12 of 13 neurons tested) and their multi-sensory properties (responsiveness to both somatosensory and visuosensory stimulation) (7 of 21 total neurons). Visuosensory stimuli that evoked the highest mean discharge rate from multi-sensory neurons were the approach and less often the withdrawal of novel or threatening objects (i.e. syringe and needle) along trajectories to and from the face. The most effective trajectories of these visual targets were aligned with the most sensitive portion of the thermal and/or mechanical cutaneous receptive field. The mean discharge rate was decreased by iterative presentation of the same novel object. . . . Familiar objects such as the experimenter's finger . . . and "moving lights" toward and away from the face (motion in depth) were ineffective visuosensory stimuli. (Dong et al. 1994, p. 550)

Particularly interesting for our purposes is the case of an HTT-EN neuron with multimodal and multisensory response properties. It has already been shown that stimulus intensity-response frequencies of the thermal nociceptive neurons that encode the magnitude of noxious thermal stimulus intensities are closely correlated with stimulus intensity-escape frequency functions. This close correlation has led us to attribute to these neurons the behaviorally significant function related to the detection of the threatening or aversive character of thermal noxious stimuli and the inducement of escape responses. So let us present in more detail the distinctive multimodal and multisensory response properties of an HTT-EN neuron and see whether they might also play a biologically and behaviorally important role for the organism:

The maximum visuosensory response was evoked by a threatening visual target (i.e., syringe and needle) that approached the face along a trajectory that was aligned with the contralateral maxillary region and was held close to the same region. . . . Because visuosensory responses may contaminate responses evoked by mechanical or thermal stimulation of the contralateral maxillary region, the monkey was temporarily blinded to the approach of the experimenter's hand and to the thermal probe resting on the face. . . . As shown . . . moving the thermal probe across the skin, brushing the hairs, and application of pressure and pinch to the skin reduced the background level of discharges in this neuron. Thermoreceptive responses . . . were evoked by applying graded thermal shifts . . . to the contralateral maxillary region from an adapting temperature of 38°C to temperatures ranging from 45 to 51°C. The thermal S-R function constructed for this neuron in area 7b showed the grading of noxious thermal intensities. . . . The maximum peak discharge frequencies in response to noxious thermal and visual stimulation were approximately equal. (Ibid., pp. 550–551)

The first notable fact about the results presented above is that they strongly confirm Robinson's and Burton's earlier finding: that in the area of granular insula and parietal operculum of the monkey's brain, there are some neurons that respond specifically to visually threatening stimuli. As I have said, this finding gave us a first clue to explain how pain asymbolia patients, who had lesions in exactly these areas of the brain, could systematically fail to respond to such stimuli by protective or avoidance behavior. However, it has not given us enough clues to understand in more precise and detailed terms why that should happen; why these patients were, although repeatedly exposed to visually threatening stimuli, unable to learn to avoid such stimuli or protect themselves from them; and, finally, why they have in some cases shown the tendency to expose themselves willingly to injurious stimuli or to approach them without fear.

The more elaborate and expanded electrophysiological and behavioral study conducted by Dong et al. may provide plausible answers to these questions. These experimenters discovered that the neurons that responded best to visually threatening stimuli were also distinctively responsive to somatosensory nociceptive stimuli. For example, the same neuron that responded to the syringe or needle approaching the face, the threatening implement being held near the face, and the application of the hot probe to the face, also responded best to noxious or damaging thermal stimuli, encoding reliably thermal stimuli intensity shifts from 47 to 51°C, and reaching its highest mean discharge frequencies at exactly the thermal stimulus intensities that evoked the most frequent and consistent escape responses in monkeys. Furthermore, Dong et al. found that the nociceptive neuron with these multisensory properties would respond to the threatening visual stimuli only if the syringe or needle was directed at, or positioned close to, its cutaneous (skin) receptive field, that is, directed at or positioned at the area on the skin of the face from which the nociceptive neuron would be activated if pinpricking or heat were applied there. Now, the fact that nociceptive neurons in area 7b are multisensory—that they respond both to somatosensory and visuosensory stimulation—points to the conclusion that the neural organization of this region of the posterior parietal cortex appears to "[integrate] nociceptive inputs with other sensory inputs in a manner that conveys information about the overall degree of threat presented to an organism" (Price 2000, p. 1771).

Of course, if this cross-sensory integration is supposed to provide "an overall sense of intrusion and threat to the physical body and self" (ibid.), it would also have to play a role in, or be closely related to, memory and learning. A further observation by Dong et al. suggests that this may well be the case. The experimenters noted that the mean discharge rate of nociceptive multisensory neurons was decreased by iterative presentations of the same novel object. The following observation by Robinson and Burton lends additional credence to the claim that these neurons are involved in memory and learning: responses to visually threatening stimuli, such as a pin, "stopped, following repeated visual presentation of the pin, or after a lapse of 10–15 minutes. However, a response could be elicited by showing the pin if this object was again used to apply a painful stimulus" (Robinson and Burton 1980, p. 101). This shows that the neural mechanism which consists of nociceptive multisensory neurons is perfectly apt to leave traces in the memory about the threatening or damaging nature of the stimuli and to ground associative learning with regard to such stimuli. As we have already seen, the mechanism actually has two basic capacities that make it suitable to play this role. First, multisensory nociceptive neurons have the capacity to encode reliably and effectively the threatening or damaging nature of the noxious somatosensory stimuli, such as a pinprick or hot probe, when they are brought near the face, and to induce avoidance behavior. Second, they are tuned to respond to novel objects whenever they are directed at or near the face of the organism, that is, when the target location or direction of motion within the visual receptive field is spatially aligned with the cutaneous receptive field (Price 2000, p. 1771). As Dong et al. have noted:

Such a neural ensemble in area 7b could conceivably work as a spatially and temporally coordinated unit to provide continuous sensory information about (1) the general location of the novel and potentially noxious stimulus in extra-personal space and its rate of motion in depth . . . and (2) the general location of a noxious stimulus in personal space and its change in magnitude. Such dynamic visual-somatic information about an approaching noxious stimulus and impending tissue damage, respectively, may be necessary for directing motor adjustments . . . to minimize body exposure and contact with the offending stimulus. (Dong et al. 1994, p. 561)

So, when an object, such as a needle or a glowing match, is initially presented to the monkey's face, the sight of the match will evoke the response of nociceptive neurons in area 7b and get them "ready" for the assessment of the potentially noxious or threatening significance of the incoming stimuli. For that to happen, the needle or glowing match must approach the face along a precise trajectory, bringing the stimuli into the cutaneous receptive field of the nociceptive neuron. Once the face is, on that precise point, encroached by the needle or the match, the nociceptive neuron will encode the harmful or damaging nature of the stimuli and induce escape behavior. This will lead to the integration of the somatosensory noxious stimulus with the visuosensory stimulus, and the latter stimulus will be associated with potentially noxious or threatening significance and will become apt to evoke escape behavior. Repeated approach and encroach of the needle or glowing match would strengthen this associative tie and, thus, foster the threatening significance of the visual stimuli as well as the frequency of escape from it. This hypothesis is supported by the fact that, in the case of nociceptive multisensory neurons, "the maximum peak discharge frequencies in response to noxious thermal and visual stimulation were approximately equal" (Dong et al. 1994, pp. 550–551). However, the mean discharge rate of nociceptive multisensory neurons dramatically decreases or stops after repeated presentations of the needle or lit match, provided the monkey never actually is pricked or burned during the series of presentations. In other words, the potentially noxious or threatening significance would eventually become disassociated from the corresponding visual stimuli and would therefore cease to evoke escape responses. As Robinson and Burton have observed, the association could be reinstated if the monkey were pricked or singed with the match.

Now that we have an insight into how the neural mechanism of nociceptive multisensory neurons in area 7b works, we are in a better position to understand why trauma to the parietal operculum and posterior insula may deprive an organism of the capacity to respond to threatening visual stimuli and to learn avoidance behavior to such stimuli. Owing to trauma to this brain region, an organism would no longer be able to integrate visuosensory stimuli with noxious somatosensory stimuli. In other words, the pinprick or heat contact that followed the visual presentation of the needle or glowing match directed at the face would simply fail to evoke the response of nociceptive neurons that encode the damaging or destructive nature of noxious mechanical and thermal stimuli and induce escape behavior. Thus, the visual presentation of the needle or glowing match would not be associated with damaging or destructive stimuli and would acquire neither the significance of threat nor the strength to elicit escape behavior by itself. Such an organism would lack the basic neural mechanism by which it could learn the potentially noxious or threatening significance of visual stimuli and avoidance behavior in response to such stimuli. As pain asymbolia patients have suffered trauma in the region of parietal operculum and posterior insula, which are exactly the seat of this mechanism, one could explain along the same lines their inability to attach potentially noxious or threatening significance to visual stimuli and to learn to avoid such stimuli. The complete absence of this capacity would also help to explain why some patients show the tendency to approach harmful objects or willingly expose themselves to them.

6 Conceptual and Theoretical Implications of Pain Asymbolia

Now that we have reviewed the neurological evidence that shows how pain asymbolia is possible, let us try to see whether and in what respect this extraordinary syndrome might be relevant to our understanding of the very concept and even the very nature and structure of pain itself. As far as these conceptual and theoretical implications are concerned, it seems that there are at least two important lessons to be learned from pain asymbolia. The first lesson is that pain, although seemingly simple and homogenous, is actually a complex experience. The sensory-discriminative, emotional-cognitive, and behavioral components typically occur together, but they can exist separately. The second lesson is that without affective, cognitive, and behavioral components, pain loses all of its representational and motivational force: it is no longer a signal of threat or damage and no longer moves one's mind and body in any way. It becomes a blunt, inert sensation, with no power to galvanize the mind and body for fight or flight. Such pain no longer serves its primary biological function. As Denny-Brown has remarked: "such patients (i.e. those with pain asymbolia) that we have seen can feel pain and can discuss it, though it is not of any biological importance to them" (1962, p. 244). In other words, for these patients, pain is no longer a biological self-defense mechanism. As the meaning of the original Latin word, *poena*, implies, pain is supposed to "punish" the organism for doing something dangerous, or for doing something that may worsen an existing injury. Without this punishment, there is no reminder or lesson to teach the creature to change its self-destructive ways. By contrast, the pain that asymbolics feel upon being harmfully stimulated comes, as they put it, to nothing, or, at best, to something that they smile or laugh at.

But how can one react to pain by smiling or laughing? What would one actually smile or laugh *at*? The main reason pain asymbolia patients laugh at the pain they feel is that they are not experiencing or perceiving it as a threat, a danger, or as damage to the integrity of their bodies. Actually, by smiling or laughing at it they are dismissing it as sign of physical damage, or at least as a threat to their physical well-being. For them, pain is a mock threat or mock danger, because in their case, nothing horrible, frightening, or awful is experienced in the pain that they feel upon being, for instance, severely pinpricked. But pinpricks, particularly severe ones, are "supposed to" evoke strongly aversive or frightening sensations. But the pain that asymbolics feel on such occasions flies in the face of these expectations. The incongruity between what is expected and what is experienced makes them smile or laugh at the pain that they feel when severely pinpricked. That the smiling and laughter displayed by asymbolia patients is specifically directed at the peculiar character of the pain that they feel during noxious stimulation, and not elicited by some other factors, is strongly supported by the fact that this strange behavior ceases abruptly when the stimulation is discontinued. However, asymbolia patients may also smile or laugh during pain testing for other reasons. Their smiles and laughter may also be understood as directed toward neurologists who are daily and repeatedly exposing them to injurious stimuli, and who would normally, as we have already said, be considered more as torturers than examiners. In other words, smiles and laughter may well be an expression of reassurance in social transactions. The patients may be communicating to the neurologists that their needle pricks or punches are experienced as mock aggression, and not real danger, so that they have actually not done anything wrong. This interpretation of the bizarre smiling or laughter displayed by asymbolia patients during pain testing is supported by the fact that these patients never get angry at examiners; they maintain a cooperative and friendly attitude toward them during the whole testing period and sometimes may even pay their respects by curtsey.

As we have seen, the fact that asymbolia patients consistently smile during the pain testing procedure is basically the outcome of their inability to perceive or experience the pain that they feel as a threat, danger, or damage to the integrity of their body and mind. However, this pain, which does not represent threat, danger, or damage to asymbolia patients and in no way alarms them, but makes them only smile or laugh, poses a gross threat to both the subjectivist and the objectivist conceptions or interpretations of the true nature and structure of human pain experience. Actually, by a quite unexpected ironical twist, it threatens to inflict irreparable theoretical damage to these conceptions of pain. At least, it threatens to remain a permanent pain in the neck for them. In order to substantiate this rather grim and pessimistic claim, I will first consider how the case of pain asymbolia might affect the viability of the subjectivist conception of pain, and I will then proceed to examine the damaging impact that it may have on the objectivist interpretation of pain.

According to the subjectivist view, the sensation of pain with its distinctive phenomenal content or quality—the "what-it-is-likeness" of pain—is the essential component of our total pain experience and plays the central or fundamental role in it. Allegedly, when this component is absent, there is no pain or pain becomes ersatz pain, despite the presence of all other components of pain experience. This is what the standard "absent qualia" argument is supposed to prove. If the qualitative sensation of pain really plays this essential or central role in pain experience, it seems that the subjectivists are committed to the claim that a sensation of pain is sufficient for somebody to be in pain. Actually, they might be tempted (or even forced) to claim that, in the case of pain asymbolia, where this component is present while all other components of pain experience are conspicuously absent, we have finally come to the very essence of pain; that the pure juice of pain quality—the what-it-is-likeness of pain—has been extracted and clearly presented. But, to the disappointment of many, myself very much included, the pure juice or essence of pain experience thus extracted has turned out to be a blunt, fleshless, inert sensation pointing to nothing beyond itself, leaving no traces in the memory and powerless to move the body and mind in any way. Moreover, when reduced to pure sensation, pain becomes the object of ridicule. In other words, the legendary question of what it is like to be in such pain, would get the following answer: it's kind of funny! But then one would be strongly inclined to say that this is not real pain, that it is only mock pain. Ironically, the case of pain asymbolia would show that what is supposed to be the essence of pain is actually merely a state of ersatz pain. To put this point in other terms, the case of pain asymbolia would quite unexpectedly prove that, contrary to the subjectivist's claims, the sensation of pain is not the essential component of our total pain experience, that it does not play any central or fundamental role in it. It could be used as an ironic sting against the following subjectivist's motto, put forward by Campbell in highly rhetorical biblical terms: "To a considerable extent, so far as many mental states go, by their qualia shall ye know them. To an even greater extent, by their qualia shall ye value them, imagine them, remember them, and fear them" (Campbell 1983, p. 136). As the case of pain asymbolia vividly and conclusively shows, when pain is reduced to pure qualia, it loses any force that would make one remember it, fear it, or esteem it as a threat or danger.

Actually, this most peculiar and bizarre reactive dissociation syndrome to be found in human pain experience, where only the sensation of pain is present, would speak strongly in favor of the Wittgensteinian beetle-in-the-box argument, purported to prove that the quality of the sensations that one feels is quite irrelevant for determining whether one is in pain. In other words, what is in the box does not matter for pain: what does matter is what one believes, how one feels (affectively, not sensorially) and acts (Wittgenstein 1968, §293). Of course, the case of pain asymbolia or the pain that one only smiles or laughs at would certainly be, as far as the crucial components of human pain experience are concerned, the best possible evidence that Wittgenstein was right when he has remarked that "a wheel that can be turned though nothing else moves with it, is not part of the mechanism" (1968, §271). It would also strongly speak the thesis of Valerie Hardcastle's book, *The Myth of Pain*, that "the sensation of pain—what most philosophers of mind focus upon as absolutely central to being in pain—is neither a particularly fundamental nor a particularly important component to our pain processing . . . for what something is like becomes less important in explaining our mind" (1999, p. 94).

However, we will have to examine more carefully whether the case of pain asymbolia would genuinely justify this resolute and conclusive verdict on the role of the sensation of pain in our total pain experience. But before we do that, we have to consider more closely how the case of pain asymbolia is supposed to affect the viability of the objectivist conception of the true nature and structure of pain. This conception of pain, the so-called perceptual or representational model of pain that was devised by naturalistically minded philosophers in order to show that, contrary to the subjectivist's claims, there is no intrinsic and irreducible felt quality or phenomenal content to pain experience—that the phenomenal content of pain can be, without remainder, analyzed in purely representational or relational terms. According to this model, the feeling of pain is just the awareness of objective bodily states of affairs: the perception or sensory representation of bodily or tissue damage. Furthermore, the pain sensory system is to be conceived as any other perceptual system, for instance, the visual or tactual system. Supposedly, the only difference is that pain represents some internal, bodily changes, whereas the latter are directed at objects in the outside world.

The first fully elaborated and explicitly stated perceptual model of pain was put forward by Pitcher:

to be aware of pain is to perceive—in particular, to feel, by means of the stimulation of one's pain receptors and nerves—a part of one's body that is in the damaged, bruised, irritated, or pathological state, or that is in the state that is dangerously close to being one or more of these kinds of states. (Pitcher 1970, p. 371)

The most recent version of the fully objectivist conception of pain is to be found in the writings of M. Tye; the only difference is that it now goes under the heading of the *representational* model or theory of pain. This model of pain is actually elaborated within the more general representational model that is supposed to apply to all experiences and feelings:

The picture that emerges from my discussion is one of the experiences and feelings as sensory representations either of the outside world or of certain sorts of internal, bodily changes. Moods, emotions, and bodily sensations, in my view, are importantly like maps of our own internal physical workings, guides to our inner body states, graphic representations of what is going on inside (and to) our skins. Perceptual experiences are representations of the same sort, but their focus is the outside world, the external terrain. (Tye 1995, p. 94)

When this general picture is applied to pain experience, we get the following representational model of pain:

My proposal, then, is that pains are sensory representations of bodily damage or disorder. More fully, they are mechanical responses to the relevant bodily changes in the same way that basic visual sensations are mechanical responses to proximate visual stimuli. In the case of pain, the receptors (known as nociceptors) are distributed throughout the body. These receptors function analogously to the receptors on the retina. They are transducers. They are sensitive only to certain changes in the tissue to which they are directly connected (typically, damage), and they convert that input immediately into symbols. Representations are then built up mechanically of internal bodily changes, just as representations are built up of external surfaces in the case of vision. These representations, to repeat, are sensory. They involve no concepts. One does not need to be able to conceptualize a given bodily disturbance in order to feel pain. And even if one can, it is not relevant, because feeling pain demands the sensory experience of that disturbance. (Ibid., pp. 113–114)

That the feeling of pain is not, by itself, the perception or representation of bodily or tissue damage, as is claimed by the perceptual or representational model, is shown by the case of pain asymbolia patients. As the large neurological and psychophysical literature on these patients shows, they are quite capable of discriminating, differentiating, and localizing the damaging or potentially damaging stimuli whenever they are applied to any part of their bodies, and they do feel pain therefrom. However, the pain that these patients feel does not represent for them any damage or potential damage to their bodies. That this is so is best proved by the fact that they consistently smile or laugh during pain testing procedures. If that is the case, one can safely claim that the sensation of pain does not carry, by itself, any representational force; that, when present alone, it comes to nothing in the sense that it in no way carries the "meaning" of physical damage or at least threat to physical well-being. So, contrary to the perceptual or representational model of pain, the feeling of pain cannot, when taken alone, be understood as the perception or representation of bodily or tissue damage. In other words, it seems that the representational force of pain is rather to be sought in the emotional-cognitive components of pain. As Chapman and Nakamura have remarked:

The strength of emotional arousal associated with an injury indicates, and expresses, the magnitude of perceived threat to the biological integrity of the individual. Within the contents of consciousness, threat is realization of a strong negative feeling state and not a coldly calculated informational appraisal. The emotional magnitude of a pain is the internal representation of the threat associated with the event that produced the pain. (1999, p. 400)

But this is something that Sherrington had observed much earlier:

With its liability to various kinds of mechanical and other damage in a world beset with dangers amid which the individual and species have to win their way in the struggle for existence we may regard nocuous stimuli as part of a normal state of affairs. It does not seem improbable, therefore, that there should under selective adaptation attach to the skin a so-to-say specific sense of its own injuries. As psychical adjunct to the reactions of that apparatus we find a strong unpleasant affective quality on the sensations they evoke. This may perhaps be a means for branding upon memory . . . a feeling from past events that have been perilously critical for the existence of the individuals of the species. In other words, if we admit that damage to such an exposed sentient organ as the skin must in the evolutionary history of animal life have been sufficiently frequent in relation to its importance, then the existence of a specific set of nerves for skin-pain seems to offer no genetic difficulty, anymore than does the clotting of blood or innate immunity to certain diseases. (1948, pp. 228–229)

Sherrington recognized that pain is a sensory submodality subserved by a physiologically specialized nociceptive neural system whose function is to detect harmful or potentially harmful stimuli and transmit the sensory information about these stimuli to higher cortical areas for final processing of their properties and significance. Actually, even before modern electrophysiological and psychophysical evidence, Sherrington anticipated the existence of nociceptive neurons that preferentially or distinctively respond to noxious stimuli. He even coined the modern term for this physiologically specialized class of neurons (Sherrington 1948, p. 229). That is why he writes that the skin has a specific sense of its own injuries. But he also realized that pain is not a simple sensory registration of noxious stimuli. That is why he speaks about the strong unpleasant affective quality of the sensations that the activity of the nociceptive apparatus evokes. It is this component of pain that leaves traces in memory about threatening, dangerous, or damaging stimuli. The affective quality is crucial for the organism to learn to protect itself by avoidance or defense. It is this affective dimension that is conspicuously missing in pain asymbolia patients, despite their intact sensory discrimination of noxious stimuli. So, to repeat the main point, although these patients feel pain, it simply does not represent threat or danger to them. To them this sensation is a mock threat that they smile or laugh at. Now, the perceptual or representational model of pain is grounded on the experiential, physiological, and psychophysical evidence that pain is, indeed, the sensory registration of damaging or potentially damaging stimuli subserved by the specialized nociceptive neural apparatus. That much is true. But the sensory registration of body or tissue injury or the sensation of pain felt at the site of such injury do not, by themselves, represent damage or threat to the subject. That much is clear from the consideration of the case of pain asymbolia. In other words, nociceptive signals may evoke the sensation of pain for sensory discrimination of harmful or potentially harmful stimuli, but they need to be processed further if the subject is to appreciate their affective and motivational valence or their behavioral significance. And that is the truth of the matter as far as human pain experience is concerned.

The study of pain asymbolia (pain without representational and motivational force) has shown the major fault of the perceptual or representational view of pain: the representational model fails to explain how pain can come to represent for the subject the threat or damage to his body; the model incorrectly locates this basic, primitive representational capacity of pain in the sensory-discriminative component, rather than in its emotional-cognitive dimensions. Closely related to this mistake is the erroneous claim, made by the advocates of the perceptual model of pain, that the pain sensory system differs from visual or tactual systems only with regard to its object of perception. To make such a claim is to disregard the fact that the pain sensory system, unlike the latter sensory systems, is also inherently endowed with characteristic affect that motivates behavior: all sensations "referred to the body itself, rather than interpreted as qualities of objects in the external world, tend to be 'tinged' with feeling," and "sense-organs which initiate sensations tinged with feeling tend to excite motor centers directly and imperatively" (Sherrington 1948, p. 267).

The failure of the perceptual or representational model of pain to capture and account for the representational force of pain reminds one of the doomed attempts to build a prosthetic pain system. The project, known as "A Practical Substitute for Pain," was devised and executed by Paul Brand to compensate for the defective pain perception of leprosy patients, congenital painlessness, diabetic neuropathy, and other nerve disorders. In a nutshell, the project had the following major goal:

We planned, in effect, to duplicate the human nervous system on a very small scale. We would need a substitute "nerve sensor" to generate signals at the extremity, a "nerve axon" or wiring system to convey the warning message, and a response device to inform the brain of the danger. One of the engineers . . . joked about the potential for profit: "If our idea works, we'll have a pain system that warns of danger but doesn't hurt. In other words, we'll have the good parts of pain without the bad!" (Brand and Yancey 1997, p. 192)

A team of electrical engineers developed transducers, slim metal disks smaller than a shirt button, to measure temperature and pressure. Sufficient pressure on these transducers would alter their electrical resistance, triggering an electrical current. The first problem was to determine what thresholds of pressure and temperature should be programmed into the sensors:

After many compromises we settled on baseline pressure and temperatures to activate the sensors, and then designed a glove and a sock to incorporate several transducers. At last we could test our substitute pain system on actual patients. Now we ran into mechanical problems. The sensors, state-of-the-art electronic miniatures, tended to deteriorate from metal fatigue or corrosion after a few hundred uses. . . . Worse, the sensors cost about $450 each and leprosy patients who took a long walk around the hospital grounds could wear out a $2,000 sock! (Ibid., pp. 193–194)

But the point is that there were even more serious problems related to the very efficacy or successful functioning of the artificial pain system:

Even when the transducers worked correctly, the entire system was contingent on the free will of the patients. We had grandly talked of retaining "the good parts of pain without the bad," which meant designing a warning system that would not hurt. First we tried a device like a hearing aid that would hum when the sensors were receiving normal pressures, buzz when they were in slight danger, and emit a piercing sound when they perceived an actual damage. But when a patient with a damaged hand turned a screwdriver too hard, and the loud warning signal went off, he would simply override it—This glove is always sending out false signals—and turn the screwdriver anyway. Blinking lights failed for the same reason. (Ibid., p. 194)

Here we have a substitute pain system that is in full accord with Tye's representational model of pain, one that allegedly provides an organism with sensory representations of bodily damage or disorder. It has specialized transducers, sensitive to damaging or potentially damaging stimuli, and they convert these inputs directly into symbols, so that representations are then built up mechanically of "tissue" or "bodily" changes. These representations are indeed sensory, as Tye is eager to emphasize: a piercing sound is emitted when an actual danger is detected, and the quality of this acoustic experience corresponds phenomenally to the quality of piercing pain. But the substitute pain system fails to perform its major substitutive function: to alarm the patient about the damaging stimuli and make him avoid them. What went wrong? The substitute pain system fails *just as the representational model of pain fails to capture the real representational force of pain*: The signals or messages that the patient receives simply do not represent to him a threat to his well-being. They are, for him, false signals, which he can ignore. This fact reminds one very much of the peculiar attitude that pain asymbolia patients have toward the sensation of pain. For these patients, the pain they feel is also a false alarm which they ignore or even smile or laugh at. We have only to remind ourselves that the wife of one of these patients reported that he had accidentally suffered a serious burn without escape or emotional reactions.

In order to rescue the substitute pain system from total uselessness and eventual ridicule, the team had to improve on its design, so that it could properly and efficiently perform its basic function:

The sobering realization dawned on us that unless we built in a quality of compulsion, our substitute system would never work. . . . Professor Tims of LSU said to me, almost in despair, "Paul, it's no use. We'll never be able to protect these limbs unless the signal really hurts."

We tried every alternative before resorting to pain, and finally concluded Tims was right: the stimulus had to be unpleasant, just as pain is unpleasant. One of Tims's graduate students developed a small battery-operated coil that, when activated, sent out an electric shock at high voltage but low current. It was harmless but painful, at least when applied to parts of the body that could feel pain.

Leprosy bacilli, favoring the cooler parts of the body, usually leave warm area such as the armpit undisturbed, and so we began taping the electric coil to patients' armpits for our tests. . . . I noticed though, that they viewed pain from our artificial sensors in a different way than pain from natural sources. They tended to see the electrical shocks as punishments for breaking rules, not as messages from an endangered body part. They responded with resentment, not an instinct of self-preservation, because our artificial system had no innate link to their sense of self. How could it, when they felt a jolt in the armpit for something happening to the hand?

I learned a fundamental distinction: a person who never feels pain is task-oriented, whereas a person who has as an intact pain system is self-oriented. The painless person may know by a signal that a certain action is harmful, but if he really wants to, he does it anyway. (Ibid., pp. 194–195)

One could say that the failure of this improved or upgraded artificial substitute pain system is even more striking, for this time pain itself—to put the matter in somewhat paradoxical but quite true terms—was used to serve as part of the substitute pain device. Tye could claim that this spectacular failure was to be expected for the simple reason that the pain elicited by the activity of artificial nociceptive sensors positioned on the hand was felt in the armpit. In other words, the pain was not the sensory representation of damage to the body part that was actually exposed to harmful stimulus—the hand—and thus the patient could not internalize it as a sign of threat or danger to that part of his body. Tye is certainly right on this point, and this is something that Brand noticed and offered as one of the explanations for the fiasco of his "painfully" upgraded substitute pain project. However, this substitute pain system could be, in principle, upgraded one step further so as to avoid the mismatch between the location of the sensation felt and the site of the body damage. For this purpose, signals coming from the "hand's" artificial nociceptive sensors and transducers in leprosy patients should be transmitted to electrodes inserted into the primary and secondary somatosensory areas of the brain, so that their activity would evoke the response of the somatotopically organized nociceptive neurons whose receptive fields are in the hand. In this way the sensation of pain evoked by the damaging mechanical or thermal stimulus applied to the hand would be projected to that body part: that is, pain would be felt as located in the hand.

Would that solve all of the problems for the construction of the fully effective substitute pain system? Would the pain, now projected or felt as located at the body part that is actually suffering damage, represent for the leprosy patient a threat or danger to the integrity of that particular part of his body? Yes, if the signals coming from "hand's" artificial nociceptive sensors and transducers were further transmitted to the cortical areas responsible for the processing of their affective and motor valence as well as their behavioral significance; but no, if there would be no such further processing. Unfortunately, even if we had such a "painful substitute pain system," it would still not function as a real pain system. The major deficiency of this, almost perfect, semiartificial pain system would be the fatal weakness that Brand found in his initial project:

Most important, we found no way around the fundamental weakness in our system: it remained under the patient's control. If the patient did not want to heed the warning from our sensors, he could always find a way to bypass the whole system. Looking back, I can point to a single instant when I knew for certain that the substitute pain project would not succeed. I was looking for a tool in the manual art workshop when Charles, one of our volunteer patients, came to replace a gasket on a motorcycle engine. . . . One of the engine bolts had apparently rusted, and Charles made several attempts to loosen it with a wrench. It did not give. I saw him put some force behind the wrench and then stop abruptly, jerking backward. The electric coil must have jolted him. . . . Charles studied the situation for a moment, then reached up under his armpit and disconnected a wire. He forced the bolt loose with a big wrench, put his hand in his shirt again, and reconnected a wire. It was then that I knew we had failed. Any system that allowed our patients freedom of choice was doomed. (Brand and Yancey 1997, pp. 195–196)

It is obvious that our hypothetical, perfect "painful substitute pain system" would be doomed for the same reason: the patient would be able to disconnect the wire at any time and keep on doing things that could injure him. This would certainly be irrational, but there would be nothing to stop these irrational acts: "The mysterious power of the human brain can force a person to STOP—something I could never accomplish with my substitute system" (ibid., p. 196). On the other hand, if the leprosy patients were equipped with a substitute mechanism that projected painlike sensations to the proper body part that were just short of painfulness, they would not be tempted to disconnect the wire, but they would still continue their self-injurious behavior. The insuperable "disconnect or unplug" dilemma that the substitute pain system faces would be miraculously solved, but at the price that the pain felt as located at the real site of the injury would not represent to leprosy patients any danger or threat, and would not make them avoid damaging or potentially damaging stimuli. In other words, they would not be tempted to disconnect a wire and bypass the whole substitute pain system for the same reason that asymbolia patients do not attach any significance to the pain that they feel upon harmful stimulation. In both cases, the pain would be accurately located, qualitatively discriminated, properly temporally registered and proportional to stimulus intensity, but it would come to nothing more than a blunt, inert sensation pointing to nothing beyond itself and in no way moving the mind or body. So, in these cases, there would be no problem related to the spatial mismatch between the site at which the sensation is felt and the site of the injury, but there would remain some quite serious and deep problems. These problems are actually related to the fundamental shortcomings of the representational model of pain: to the fact that this model is basically deficient as the conceptual model of pain and that it implicitly presupposes a too simplistic and inadequate picture of the neural mechanism that is supposed to subserve human pain experience.

The representational model of pain is essentially grounded on the idea of simple sensory registration of pain as a message. The message is unpacked as the sensory representation of bodily damage or disorder, or is supposed to carry, in strictly sensory terms, information about such damage or disorder. The neural mechanism of pain presupposed by this model is the one given by classical neurophysiology: that of nociception, noxious signaling, and sensory registration of pain as a predominantly bottom-up, unidirectional, sequential type of processing. But, as consideration of the case of pain asymbolia has convincingly shown, the sensation of pain does not carry by itself any message or representation of bodily damage, if nociceptive signals are not further or in parallel processed for their affective and motor valence as well as for their behavioral significance. The classical sensory neurophysiological view of pain, as well as the representational model of pain which is grounded on it, is faced with the following theoretical problems or perplexities:

This position has major problems in explaining how a sensory experience can contribute so powerfully to suffering: why pain "hurts" is still unclear. Also, this approach cannot address the knotty problem that challenges consciousness researchers—how do signals of tissue trauma make their way into consciousness? (Chapman, Nakamura, and Flores 2000, p. 28)

An important aspect of the puzzle mentioned above can be dispelled if the more complex and veridical picture of the neural mechanism that subserves human pain experience is taken into account. As we have already seen, the representational model of pain, as well as the classical sensory neurophysiological picture of pain on which it is grounded, has every right to claim that pain is subserved by the physiologically specialized nociceptive neural system whose function is to detect harmful or potentially harmful stimuli and to transmit the sensory information about these stimuli to higher cortical areas for final processing of their properties and significance. However, the information about the noxious or potentially noxious stimuli, or at least the information related to intensity, is transmitted at the thalamic level through parallel routes simultaneously activating various spatially separate cortical and subcortical areas responsible for feature-extraction, affective evaluation, attention attraction, and motor processing of the incoming nociceptive signals. Coghill and his research team have recently conducted a detailed neuroimaging study in order to determine which cortical and subcortical regions of the brain are involved in the processing of pain intensity: that crucial factor for the assessment of the danger or threat that noxious or potentially noxious stimuli carry for the integrity of the body and mind. The results of this study are summarized in the following general way:

Multiple regression analysis of the functional imaging data revealed that a number of cerebral cortical and subcortical areas exhibited significant, graded changes in activation linearly related to subjects' perceptions of pain intensity. The findings from the multiple regression analysis are independently supported by comparisons of PET scans at each stimulus temperature with the resting state. In most areas, innocuous (35°C) and threshold (46°C) stimulation produced minimal differences from rest.

However, as stimulus temperature increased to 48° and 50°C, monotonic increases in activation were evident in multiple brain areas. (Coghill et al. 1999, p. 1936)

In the discussion of Coghill's results, the basic findings are presented in a more specific and precise way. The present findings confirm in a fully quantitative manner that pain intensity is processed in a highly distributed manner. This distributed mechanism encompasses a number of functionally distinct regions that all exhibit activation that is closely related to perceived stimulus intensity. These include brain areas typically thought to be important in (1) somatosensory processing: SI, SII, and the posterior insular cortex; (2) motor processing: cerebellum, putamen/globus pallidus, supplementary motor cortex, ventral premotor cortex, and the anterior cingulate cortex; (3) affective processing: anterior cingulate cortex and insular cortex; (4) attentional processing: anterior cingulate cortex, primary somatosensory cortex, and the ventral premotor cortex; and (5) autonomic function: anterior cingulate cortex and anterior insular cortex.

Multiple, converging lines of evidence indicate that this distributed processing of pain intensity information rests on a parallel infrastructure of nociceptive transmission. First, anatomic evidence indicates that information about noxious stimulus intensity may be transmitted independently from thalamic sites to cerebral cortical areas such as SI, SII, the insular cortex, the anterior cingulate cortex, the supplementary motor cortex, and the ventral premotor cortex. Second, neurological evidence confirms that these multiple thalamocortical pathways are functionally relevant. Discrete injuries of either SI, SII, anterior cingulate cortex, or the insula fail to abolish conscious awareness of pain intensity, although other aspects of processing may be disrupted somewhere. Thus serial transmission of nociceptive information through any one of these cerebral cortical areas is not obligatory for a conscious awareness of the intensity of painful stimulus (Coghill et al. 1999, pp. 1939–1940).

The picture of the neural mechanism of pain that works as a parallel distributed mechanism gives us a clue about how to approach the problems or puzzles that seem to be completely intractable within the main premises of the representational model of pain. How does sensory experience contribute to suffering? Why does pain *hurt*? How can the sensory representation, which is and should be hedonically neutral, give rise to dislike and strong aversive reactions? How do signals of tissue trauma make their way into consciousness? Once we realize that nociceptive signals about damaging or potentially damaging stimuli are transmitted in parallel for simultaneous sensory-discriminative and emotional-cognitive processing, the mystery is dispelled, because the signals are simultaneously processed for both their painfulness and their pain character. To put this point into more precise terms, the aversive valence and biological significance of nociceptive signals is processed in parallel and simultaneously with the processing of the location at which the pain sensation is to be projected and its intensity and qualitative character decided. That the mechanism is working as a parallel-distributed mechanism, and not as a serial one, is proved by the cases of pain asymbolia and pain affect without pain sensation. The first case shows that the registration and the processing of sensory features of nociceptive signals can be successfully accomplished without any processing of their aversive valence and biological significance. The second case shows that nociceptive signals can be registered and processed for their aversive valence and biological significance without any processing of their sensory features. Of course, except in these two cases of radical disconnections between the cortical and subcortical areas of the brain responsible for the sensory-discriminative and emotional-cognitive dimensions of pain, they are working reciprocally and interactively, rather than independently. That is why, phenomenologically, they appear to us in homogenous, gestalt guise—as they should, if pain is to serve its major biological purpose. Pain must appear so to us if it is to have, to use Sherrington's terminology, preeminent intensity of feeling and, consequently, of action. So the following remark by Millan is highly justified and should always be kept in mind:

Nevertheless, it would be simplistic to impose an absolute dissociation between the sensory-discriminative and emotional-cognitive dimensions of pain. These aspects should be regarded as complementary and as operating reciprocally and interactively rather than independently. Further, a "pain center" or "pain centers" may not, as such, exist. Rather, a matrix of cerebral structures and multiple, parallel thalamocorticolimbic networks synergistically contributes to the global experience of pain. (Millan 1999, p. 40)

7 Pain Quality and Painfulness without Pain

As I have said, the case of pain asymbolia seems to lend full support to the radical antisubjectivist claim that the sensation of pain or pain quality plays no important role in our total pain experience and that what really matters is only how we respond affectively, what we believe, and how we act. But as Valerie Hardcastle has quite rightly warned, dissociation syndromes in human pain experience cannot be used to show conclusively that any one component or dimension is central to or essential for pain (1999, p. 94). This warning should certainly be taken seriously regarding that most radical reactive dissociation syndrome, pain asymbolia. The only conclusion that one is entitled to draw from the consideration of this syndrome is that pain sensation comes to nothing when it is disconnected from its affective, cognitive, and motor aspects. This conclusion does not imply that pain quality is irrelevant, or that even in its complete absence an experience could still be a pain experience. It is obviously the triggering point which sets the machinery to "go," and it sets apart the machinery that wears its sign from those that are similar to it, but do not carry its signature. In other words, the role of the distinctive quality of pain is, first, to distinguish sensory pain from so-called mental pain or suffering; second, to set pain apart from other unpleasant sensations by its distinctive quality; third, to differentiate it from other, phenomenally similar sensations and give unity to the sensations that pertain to the sensory modality of pain.

As far as the first role is concerned—that of distinguishing sensory pain from nonphysical pain or mental hurt—it is sufficient to quote the following remark by Sherrington: "The disagreeableness of a vivid color contrast or of discordant notes is akin to pain but is it really a degree of 'physical pain'? Is it strictly expressible as a fraction of the agonizing torture of a scalded limb?" (1900, p. 968). To make this point even more vivid and convincing, Sherrington agrees with Foster's observation that "the pain which we feel when the finger is cut is a wholly different thing from the pain given to the most delicately musical ear by even the most horrible discord" (ibid.). The point of this comparison is to show that there is a sensory quality in the first case that is missing in the second case; and that it is exactly the lack of this quality that differentiates the pain of listening to poorly played music from the pain of a lacerated finger, however unpleasant both experiences may be.

And this brings us to the second important role that the distinctive quality of pain plays in our total pain experience: the role of differentiating pain from other unpleasant sensations from which it can only be distinguished by its sensory quality or modality. Nausea is one such case; but as Sherrington rightly observed, "some sensations of taste, e.g. bitter, sour, certain odors, possess an unpleasant character—a 'negative tone'— almost at the limn of the sensible intensity of the stimulus. Here the disagreeableness seems to be allied, not to the intensity, but to the 'timbre' or 'color' or quality of the sensation" (1900, p. 967). As far as the experimental evidence for this claim is concerned, it is worth noting that Henry Head's experiments led him to distinguish between the sensory quality of pain and the feeling-tone of discomfort which usually accompanies it. Head examined the effect of an electric current on a leg which was "totally insensitive to painful stimulation of all kinds, in consequence of an intramedullary lesion," and he found that "so long as tactile sensibility remains perfect [the patient] will complain bitterly of the discomfort caused by this form of stimulation" (Head 1920, p. 405). Experiments with two patients "showed that the movement of withdrawal seemed to be almost as violent when a current of known strength was applied to the analgesic as to the normal leg"; and one patient said that the sensation produced was "a kind of exaggerated tickling more unpleasant than pain" (ibid.). Both patients were firm in their assertions that the sensation was not painful; and yet an observer watching their behavior would suppose they were experiencing intolerable pain. As Roger Trigg has observed, situations like these "seem to show that the emotional component of pain can be combined with some types of sensations and yet neither the resulting complex nor the 'bare sensation' (if such thing is possible) be called 'pain'" (1970, p. 23). As Ryle wrote in *The Concept of Mind*:

It should be mentioned that "pain," in the sense in which I have pains in my stomach, is not the opposite of "pleasure." In this sense, a pain is a sensation of special sort, which we ordinarily dislike having. (1973, p. 105)

Pain is indeed a sensation of special sort. It is a sensory submodality or experiential determinable that gives unity to sensations that carry its mark and sets them apart from sensations of other modalities that are qualitatively similar to pain. For example, the pain that one feels upon mechanical or thermal stimulation can be dull or sharp, stinging or burning. That is, the sharpness or dullness as well as the stinging or burning qualities of the sensation may correspond to qualitative differences *within* the modality of pain, designating different kinds of pain within the same genus. Or, to put it another way: sharp pain and dull pain, like stinging pain and burning pain, are experiential determinates of the sensation of pain. But differences between sensations that are felt as sharp or dull, as well as those that are felt as stinging or burning, may also correspond to the intramodal differences within the sense of touch or the sense of temperature. That means that one can discriminate the mechanical or thermal stimuli as sharp or dull or as stinging or burning and yet not feel pain, because the sensations felt do not carry the quality pain. In order to be felt as painful, these sensations have to pertain to the modality of pain; otherwise, the subject will not feel pain despite the fact that he feels sensations that he discriminates as sharp or dull, or as stinging or burning. So, it seems that the concept of pain quality or the concept of pain modality really plays the important role of giving unity to sensations that fall under the heading of pain and setting them apart from those that are qualitatively similar but of different modality: of something that serves to embrace them so as to mark their territory and boundaries.

That this is so may be vividly illustrated and clearly documented by the consideration of clinical syndromes that are in most behavioral and affective respects similar to pain asymbolia, but differ from it in one crucial or decisive phenomenal respect: they lack the very feeling of pain which is so conspicuously present in the latter syndrome. The syndromes that I have in mind include the case of so-called congenital insensitivity to pain or, better, congenital analgesia, and the case of acquired analgesia due to brain trauma. The interesting thing about these syndromes is that analgesia—loss of sensitivity to pain—is not always followed by anesthesia—total loss of sensation in all or part of the body. Patients suffering from congenital analgesia, similarly to pain asymbolia patients, do not show common reactions to noxious or potentially noxious stimuli:

The examination of pain reaction was done in many ways. All the usual noxious stimuli—pricking with a pin, electric shocks, pressure on sensitive parts, hair-pulling, burning, and pinching—were used. Other tests included . . . tests for the production of muscle pain, the production of "cold pain" from immersion of the hand in cold water . . . and the production of headache by injection of histamine phosphate.

Absence of reaction in nearly all these tests means that the patients did not show the usual behavior of withdrawal, attack, wincing, crying out, or reporting pain . . . Also, the most striking evidence of insensitivity to pain rests usually in the patient's past history of indifference to everyday noxious stimuli, many of them much more damaging than could be administered for purposes of examination. (McMurray 1955, pp. 124–125)

Like pain asymbolia patients, not all congenital analgesics are insensitive to noxious stimuli:

[These patients] can detect, identify, and localize noxious stimuli and can easily differentiate them from other stimuli. McMurray's [patient] . . . states that, when a hypodermic needle is inserted into her skin, she feels it penetrating the tissue layers but does not "feel pain." Stimuli such as pinprick and cutaneous shock and heat produce the report of a pricking or sharp quality, but she does not describe this quality as "painful." In fact, since this S can discriminate the sharp quality of heat stimulation, McMurray was able to establish in the patient a "threshold" close to the normal heat pain threshold. Similarly, [other authors] have reported that their Ss had no difficulty differentiating and localizing a nociceptive stimulus; they could, for example, easily discriminate between the blunt and pointed end of a pin and had no difficulty localizing the pinprick. (Barber 1959, p. 443)

So it seems that the major difference between pain asymbolia patients and sufferers of congenital analgesia is that only the former feel pain. That is, only asymbolics have sensations with the quality of pain. Patients suffering from congenital analgesia can discriminate the sharp, pricking qualitative character of noxious mechanical and thermal stimuli, but they do not feel pain, because their sensations have no pain quality and simply are not sensations of pain. That again shows that the role of pain quality or separate pain modality is to unite and distinguish the class of sensations that fall under the heading or genus of pain.

The concept of a pain quality or the sensation of pain is also needed for diagnostic purposes to make distinctions between clinical syndromes which are outwardly similar in terms of the lack of appropriate behavioral and affective reactions to painful stimuli but are, nevertheless, phenomenologically different. As Trelles has observed, pain asymbolia can be understood "as analgotimia with algognosia while congenital analgesia . . . is at the same time a case of analgotimia with analgognosia" (Trelles 1978, p. 18). That is to say, in the first case, one is not in pain but nevertheless feels pain, while in the second case, one neither is in pain nor feels pain.

The importance of the distinction between feeling pain and being in pain for clinical diagnostic purposes can also be seen in the case of the patient studied by Masson et al. As a result of trauma to the posterior insula, the parietal operculum, and the supramarginal gyrus, this patient lost all sensation on the left side of the body:

The most spectacular deficiency was related to pain sensibility which was completely lost: pinprick was not perceived and the same holds for vigorous nociceptive stimulations . . . the patient denied all painful perception, made no movements of escape and had no appropriate grimacing at all. (Masson et al. 1991, p. 668)

However:

[on the right side of the body] the patient was perfectly able to discriminate the touch of the needle, but the application of strong nociceptive stimulation didn't evoke any painful sensation and didn't elicit any reaction of escape. The patient who was warned about the painful character of the stimulations that are going to be applied manifested no emotional reaction. (Ibid., p. 670)

Masson et al. diagnosed their patient as suffering from pain asymbolia. But it is quite obvious that this patient does not meet the stringent diagnostic criteria for pain asymbolia put forward by Berthier, Starkstein, and Leiguarda. Pain asymbolia patients have no deficit in pain perception on either side of their bodies, although they have absent or inadequate motor and emotional responses to painful stimuli applied anywhere on the body surface. Consequently, the case of the patient studied by Masson et al. should actually have been treated as a case of acquired severe hemianesthesia on the left side of the body and hemianalgesia on the right side of the body.

The cases of this patient and of other patients suffering from congenital analgesia not followed by anesthesia are, in many respects, observationally indistinguishable from the cases of pain asymbolia patients. Characteristic of all of these cases is the absence of adequate motor and emotional reactions to harmful stimuli. Furthermore, this deficit can have equally disastrous consequences for the patients. We must remember that pain asymbolia patients, like patients with congenital analgesia, may suffer serious injuries without attempting to avoid them or displaying any emotional reactions. However, there is a crucial and decisive phenomenological difference between these patients, which is that only the former feel pain on such occasions: neither group is *in* pain, but the asymbolics do have sensations that have pain quality. So, it seems that the distinction between feeling pain and being in pain is viable, and that the concept of pain quality is indispensable to give unity to the sensations that carry its stamp and thereby set them apart from those that may be similar to them but are of a different modality.

In his famous dialogue, *Meno*, Plato remarked that the major task of science (i.e., philosophy) is to cut nature at its joints: that is, to make distinctions that correspond to the real distinctions in the world; or, to put the same point into other words, to not lump together phenomena that are fundamentally distinct and that, accordingly, need to be given different descriptions and explanations. The same holds for mental phenomena: we should not lump together clinical syndromes that may be observationally almost indistinguishable, but that nonetheless differ in fundamental phenomenological respects: in this case, in the absence or presence of the very sensation of pain. At this point, verificationists and antirealists—both of the parochial and urbane variety—will protest vigorously in order to defend their basic epistemological and metaphysical convictions. They will resolutely claim that distinctions that make no observational difference should be dismissed or discounted. Now, there might be something in this epistemologically and metaphysically motivated demand, but even so, there *is* also an important behavioral difference between pain asymbolia patients and those who suffer from congenital or acquired analgesia. Unlike the former, the latter never smile or laugh during pain testing procedures. This can be best explained by the fact that, in their case, unlike in the case of those with pain asymbolia, there is no feeling of pain that serves as a false alarm or mock threat to prompt the patient's amusement or laughter. So, in this case, phenomenological differences are, indeed, reflected in observable behavioral differences. The main point is that these crucial behavioral differences are caused by, and are to be explained by, the corresponding phenomenological differences, or by the simple fact that only asymbolia patients feel pain or have the sensation of pain when they are harmfully stimulated.

As we have seen, there is plenty of clinical, experimental, and experiential evidence that proves that the sensation of pain (pain quality) plays an important role in the total human experience of pain. To repeat, its central role is to distinguish pain sensations from nonphysical pain, and from other unpleasant sensations, as well as from other sensations that may be qualitatively similar to it but are of different modality. If that is the case, then this evidence suggests that this fundamental role of the sensation of pain may be used to undermine one of the most powerful antisubjectivist arguments for the functionalist interpretation of pain experience. This argument is the only one which allows functionalism to move from a perpetual, tedious defense of its position to an unexpectedly vigorous offense. The main target of this argument is the phenomenal character of sensations which is so often felt to be missing from the functionalist account. The point of the argument is to prove that— contrary to deeply rooted subjectivist intuitions—this allegedly missing phenomenal element, even when present and fully recognized, plays no essential role in establishing the type-identity conditions for states. Ironically enough, pain—that paradigm case of a sensory state often considered to be, in principle, resistant to functionalist analysis or decomposition—is taken to prove this point. The functionalist claims, on introspective grounds, that various phenomena described as "pain" have qualitatively different sensations, and that—consequently— there is no common felt quality that can give unity to pain or constitute its type-identity. From this, the functionalist concludes that the unity or type-identity of pain lies solely in the common or similar stimulus-response pattern displayed in all qualitatively different instantiations of this sensory state. This argument was originally advanced by the Churchlands:

Consider the wide variety of qualia willfully lumped together in common practice under the heading of pain. Compare the qualitative character of a severe electric shock with that of a sharp blow to the kneecap; compare the character of hands dully aching from making too many snowballs with the piercing sensation of a jet engine heard at very close range; compare the character of a frontal headache with the sensation of a scalding pot grasped firmly. It is evident that what unites sensations of such diverse characters is the similarity in their functional roles. The sudden onset of any of them prompts an involuntary withdrawal of some sort. Our reaction to all of them is immediate dislike, and the violence of the dislike increases with the intensity and duration of the sensation. All of them are indicators of physical trauma of some kind, actual or potential. All of them tend to produce shock, impatience, and vocal reactions of familiar kinds. Plainly, these collected causal features are what unite the class of painful sensations, not some uniform quale, invariant across cases. (Churchland and Churchland 1981, pp. 125–126)

A similar argument, devised to show that the essence of pain is describable not in qualitative or phenomenal terms but rather in functional terms, is found in Michael Tye's book, *The Metaphysics of Mind*:

Functionalists have been quick to point out that pain is not a state the essence of which can be defined in phenomenal terms. Pains vary enormously in how they feel. Consider, for example, the pain of a burn, a headache, a very loud noise to the ear, a pinprick, a bee sting. Nonetheless, such pains do at least typically elicit the same mental reaction, namely dislike. This leads to the thought that the characteristic of typically eliciting a reaction of dislike is part of the essence of pain. I say "part" here because there are other effects (and causes) that seem to many philosophers no less important to the classification of a given state as pain. Consider, for example, such typical causal relationships as these: resulting from bodily damage or trauma; giving rise to worry and distress; causing attempts to move the body away from the damaging stimulus; causing nursing of the relevant part of the body.

Functionalists have asserted that causal relationships like these exhaust the essence of pain. According to functionalism, any sensory state type (and indeed any mental state type) can be defined via its causal connections with certain standard stimuli, certain other types of mental states, and certain standard behavioral responses. (Tye 1989, p. 91)

That pain, because of its qualitative variety, cannot be given unity through its common felt quality, is also argued by Norton Nelkin:

Though introspection cannot resolve many of the problems in this area, an appeal to the reader's introspection on this issue seems entirely legitimate: consider the significant differences among phenomena we do call pain phenomena (those experienced when cut, when suffering a toothache, or when having a headache). It is hard to understand what feeling they all share in common such that they are all pains. (Nelkin 1994, p. 329)

The argument advanced by the Churchlands, Tye, and Nelkin that there is no common or uniform felt quality that would unite the class of pain sensations may, at first sight, appear convincing or even conclusive, because it relies on the uncontestable introspective evidence that there is a striking qualitative difference between sensations that fall under the heading of pain. But this argument will loosen its grip to the point of full release the moment we realize that the qualitative differences between pain sensations that the Churchlands, Tye, and Nelkin refer to and base their argument on, are actually intramodal differences within the modality of pain: that is, the qualitatively distinct sensations of sharp pain and dull pain or sensations of stinging and burning pain are experiential *determinates* of the experiential *determinable* modality of pain. As I have shown, patients who are unable to feel pain upon noxious stimulation may, nevertheless, be able to discriminate between sharp and dull or between stinging and burning sensations from noxious mechanical or thermal stimuli. Here, the qualitative differences in the sensations are in intramodal differences within the modality of touch or temperature perception. In other words, if a sharp or dull sensation is to be felt as pain, it has to carry the mark of pain quality or pain modality. It is this quality that unites pain sensations and sets them apart from other sensations that may be phenomenally similar to them but are of a different modality. Furthermore, the common felt quality that gives unity to pain sensations or makes them a separate class of sensations is also what sets them apart from other unpleasant sensations. Tye's claim "that the characteristic of typically eliciting a reaction of dislike is part of the essence of pain" is not only incomplete or deficient in functionalist terms, but also wanting in phenomenal terms, because it ignores the fact that there are other unpleasant sensations besides pain, and that pain is distinguished from them by its unique and distinctive felt quality.

A similar remark was made by Roger Trigg when he considered possible answers to the question, "Why do you dislike that sensation?"

To be told that it is because it is unpleasant is to have the dislike of the sensation merely reaffirmed. The answer "Because it hurts" or "Because it is painful" not only rules out many unpleasant types of sensation but explains why we dislike that sensation. Similarly the statement that a sensation "is unpleasant, but isn't painful" is not a contradiction. It tells us that the sensation may be disliked, but nevertheless does not have that distinctive and insistent quality which marks off pain from other sensations. (Trigg 1970, p. 26)

This again proves that, contrary to the antisubjectivist claims of the Churchlands, Tye, and Nelkin, the role of pain quality or the concept of a separate pain modality is to unite and demarcate the class of sensations that fall under the heading or genus of pain. It also shows how the common and distinctive felt quality of pain is the essential component of our total pain experience and why that experience is not pain experience when that component is missing. As far as the functionalist arguments against subjectivism are concerned, the most that one can claim is that pain sensation comes to nothing when it is disconnected from the corresponding affective, cognitive, and motor components of our total pain experience, as demonstrated by the plight of pain asymbolia patients. Once we make the distinction between feeling pain and being in pain, and allow that one can feel pain without being in pain, it becomes obvious and undisputable that the painfulness of pain experience depends on its affective, cognitive, and motor components. However, the affective, cognitive, and motor machinery that produces whatever painfulness there is to pain must, nevertheless, wear on its sleeve the signature of pain sensation in order to count as genuine pain. So, it seems that not only must we allow that pain without painfulness is possible, we must also make room for the opposite possibility: painfulness without pain. In other words, we might now be willing to accept that it is conceivable, and thus possible, for someone to be in pain without feeling pain. The point is that, as in the case of pain without painfulness, we need not exert ourselves in constructing bold imaginary scenarios or far-fetched thought experiments in order to see whether painfulness without pain is possible; there is incontestable clinical evidence that such cases exist, and showing that something is actual is the shortest and most reliable way to prove that it is, indeed, possible.

The case we are interested in was only recently disclosed. The phenomenon of interest has been described as pain affect without pain sensation. This bizarre condition was discovered during the neurological testing of a patient with selective lesions of the right primary (SI) and secondary (SII) somatosensory cortices, exactly those areas of the brain that are thought to be responsible for the processing of the sensory-discriminative components of pain, that is, the precise spatial localization, temporal registration, intensity calibration, and qualitative characterization of the sensations of pain evoked by noxious or potentially noxious stimuli:

> While sensory examination of the patient's right side was within normal limits, left-sided examination revealed hypoaesthesia of foot, leg and face and anesthesia of hand and arm. . . . In particular, thermal stimuli did not evoke any sensation. (Ploner, Freund, and Schnitzler 1999, p. 212)

When controlled, selective thermonociceptive stimuli were applied by means of cutaneous laser stimulation, the following results were obtained:

> Pain thresholds were 200 mJ for right hand and both feet. Evoked pain sensations were characterized as "pinprick-like" and were well localized within 2–3 cm. For left hand, up to an intensity of 600 mJ, no pain sensation could be elicited. However, at intensities of 350 mJ and more, the patient spontaneously described a "clearly unpleasant" intensity dependent feeling emerging from an ill-localized and extended area "some-

where between fingertips and shoulder," that he wanted to avoid. The fully cooperative and eloquent patient was completely unable to further describe quality, localization, and intensity of the perceived stimulus. Suggestions from a given word list containing "warm," "hot," "cold," "touch," "burning," "pinprick-like," "slight pain," "moderate pain," and "intense pain" were denied nor did the patient report any kind of paraesthesia. . . . Reaction times to laser stimuli on the right hand showed a bimodal distribution with medians at 400 ms and 1000 ms. By contrast, stimulation of the left hand yielded exclusively long-latency responses with a median at 1426 ms. (Ibid., p. 213)

As the authors of this study pointed out, their results demonstrated, for the first time in humans, "a loss of pain sensation with preserved pain affect" (ibid., p. 211). With regard to the general implications of this phenomenon, related to the assessment of the proper role and place of sensory-discriminative and affective-motivational components in human pain experience, the authors had this to say:

In the patient reported here, clinical examination and cutaneous laser stimulation revealed prolonged reaction times to painful laser stimuli, an elevated pain threshold, loss of sensory-discriminative pain component and preserved motivational-affective dimension of pain. This clear perceptual dissociation was paralleled by an anatomical dissociation between affected lateral pain system and spared medial pain system. This pattern of impairment shows the essential role of SI and/or SII for the sensory-discriminative aspects of pain perception in humans. By contrast, detection of and reaction to painful stimuli as well as pain affect do obviously not require integrity of SI and SII. Nevertheless, damage to SI and SII produced hypoalgesia in our patient, suggesting interaction between medial and lateral pain system in normal pain experience. (Ibid., p. 213)

In this case of painfulness without pain, we have a clear and vivid picture of what pain experience comes to when it is deprived of its sensory-discriminative component while its affective and behavioral components are kept intact. The subject who has lost the sensory-discriminative capacities of pain is no longer able to precisely localize noxious stimuli applied to his body. The most that he can do is refer to a diffuse area "somewhere between fingertips and shoulder." This means that one of the primary biological functions of pain has been lost, namely, the accurate localization of harmful or potentially harmful stimuli:

Such function appears reserved for pain as a signal of noxious challenge to the body surface which needs to be well localized for the purposes of removal of agent, projection of the injured site or inhibition by gentle rubbing or scratching. (Ochoa and Torebjörk 1989, p. 593)

The second major deficiency is the absence of the capacity for precise temporal registration of damaging or potentially damaging thermal stimuli. The subject displayed prolonged reaction times to painful laser stimuli, which suggests that he has lost the capacity to instantly detect the noxious stimulus, which may have disastrous consequences. A dangerous stimulus could inflict damage to the body long before the affective and motor machinery is recruited for self-preservation. The patient's inability to precisely determine the intensity of the noxious stimulus also means that he has lost another vital function of pain. The subject was unable to describe the intensity of the perceived stimulus with any of the words suggested to him: "slight pain," "moderate pain," or "intense pain." So one can say that he is unable to evaluate the extent and significance of the threat that the noxious or potentially noxious stimulus presents. The fact that the subject could not specify in any way the quality of the perceived stimulus suggests that no information about the character of the stimulus was available to him. He denied any specification of the sensation felt as "warm," "hot," "cold," "touch," "burning," or "pricking-like," so he could not, on qualitative grounds, determine whether the sensation felt was of pain or not; nor could he on qualitative grounds determine the nocuous or innocuous character of the stimulus. His dislike of the feeling of cutaneous laser stimulation and his accompanying wish to avoid it were not motivated by the quality and intensity of the sensation felt, by that distinctive and insistent quality which distinguishes pain from other sensations. Rather, the patient was motivated by the pure unpleasantness of the experience. Paradoxically enough, in this bizarre case of pain affect without pain sensation, his only answer to the query—"Why do you dislike that sensation?"—was "Because it is unpleasant." It is true that to give such an answer is really to give no answer, but merely to reaffirm one's dislike of the sensation. It tells us nothing new. But the point is that in this case, this was all the information available to the subject.

What can the cases of pain without painfulness and painfulness without pain teach us about the concept of pain or, more to the point, about the experience of pain? Should they be treated as cases of genuine pain or just as extreme aberrations that tell us nothing about the true nature of the phenomenon that we are interested in? Well, on the one hand, there is pure pain sensation, and on the other hand, there is the pure feeling of unpleasantness, defying any further sensory specification. In the first case, pain comes to nothing, because it does not carry any meaning for the subject and does not move (*emotio*) him. In the second case, pain comes to such sensory indeterminacy that it loses informativeness about the location, intensity, and source, or character of harmful stimuli. So, as far as the two basic components of human pain experience are concerned, it is obvious that both of them are necessary, but neither of them is a sufficient condition for pain. The two phenomena give us real pain only when they work together. This is how it should be, if Mother Nature devised the pain system to serve its primary biological function: to give an organism information concerning threatening or damaging stimuli and simultaneously to move it to self-preservation.

Among the reactive dissociation syndromes, pain asymbolia offers the most striking and persuasive evidence that it is possible to be indifferent to pain. It is, of course, also the most vivid and dramatic evidence of what would happen to us if we were indifferent to pain; for it shows quite clearly that we would simply no longer be able to protect the integrity of our bodies and minds. As I have argued, pain asymbolia is the only reactive dissociation syndrome that is a clear case of total indifference to pain. Moreover, it is the only clear-cut case in which pain is no longer felt as unpleasant. If one peruses all the putative cases of indifference to pain cited in the scientific literature, it turns out that there are various ways in which people can be "indifferent" to pain. In other words, the kind of indifference expressed by the statements, "I don't care," "I don't mind," or "It doesn't bother me," may differ with regard to its scope and object. A patient might say such a thing because she no longer experiences pain as unpleasant, but that is not the only possible reason. Finally, these cases of putative indifference to pain may differ with regard to their physical causes and their neurological and psychological causes. In order to prove this point, I will at some length compare the indifference to pain displayed in pain asymbolia patients with the indifference of lobotomized, cingulotomized, and morphinized patients. But first, all of these cases of real indifference to pain, whatever their scope, objects, and causes, should be set apart from those cases which are often mistaken for indifference to pain.

In the clinical literature, some cases of absent or atypical pain behavior are inadequately and misleadingly described as indifference to pain, when they are actually cases of indifference to noxious or harmful stimuli, rather than to pain, per se. As the term implies, in order to be *indifferent to pain*, one should be able to feel it, but not mind it, and also should lack any tendency to react negatively to it. On the other hand, one can be indifferent to noxious or harmful stimuli *because* these stimuli do not hurt. In the first case, indifference presupposes the presence of pain or pain-feeling, while in the second case, indifference is due to the absence of pain from stimuli that would normally be painful. Transient indifference to noxious stimuli is displayed under various unusual conditions:

For example, severe noxious stimulation may go unnoticed during extreme excitement, anger, or fear, as in combat or sports. Absence of reaction may also be found in the apathy of extreme depression. States of dissociation, like hysteria and hypnosis, show unusual indifference to noxious stimuli as a main characteristic. Reports of self-mutilation involving severe bodily damage are not uncommon in psychotic episodes. (McMurray 1955, p. 121)

Permanent global indifference to noxious stimuli is characteristic of patients who suffer from congenital universal analgesia or, as it is sometimes called, congenital insensitivity to pain. As the latter term implies, these patients actually lack pain or pain-feeling throughout the body. But the loss or absence of pain upon stimulation which would normally be painful need not mean, indeed in these patients does not mean, an inability to detect or recognize these stimuli. As I said earlier, these patients are quite able to discriminate between sharp and dull stimuli or between stinging and burning stimuli. In other words, loss of pain or pain-feeling need not involve or imply complete somatosensory loss. The patients we are interested in have sensations when they are noxiously stimulated, but the sensations evoked by this kind of stimulation are sensations of touch or of heat, not of pain. In their case, there is a mismatch between the stimulus mode and the response mode, which leads to the loss of specificity of a sensory modality. In other words, the original modality of sensations evoked by noxious stimuli is normally painful, but in cases of congenital analgesia these stimuli evoke nonpainful sensations.

The fact that patients suffering from congenital analgesia or insensitivity to pain are, nevertheless, able to detect and discriminate noxious stimuli as sharp or dull is exactly the source of deep confusion and serious misunderstanding that have led some authors to claim that these syndromes would be better treated as cases of congenital indifference to pain. Critchley, who has reviewed the largest sample of reports on patients considered to suffer from congenital insensitivity to pain, has claimed that the alternative label, "congenital indifference to pain," is preferable, because it avoids "the ambiguity of the term 'sensitivity' which might unwittingly suggest some loss of pain-feeling" (1956, p. 741). But that the loss or absence of pain or sensation of pain is the distinctive mark of the patients that Critchley studied stems from the very results of pain testing which he himself presented. Out of seven patients, not one patient had a headache upon histamine injection, two had a sense of throbbing, and three experienced flushing with subjective warmth. Out of ten patients, not one patient felt pain or discomfort upon prolonged muscle ischemia, and only one experienced a light feeling. Electric shock failed to cause pain in four patients and they did not object to faradic stimulation (ibid., p. 740). However, for Critchley, the decisive thing is that patients, who are in no way mentally retarded, hysterical, or psychotic, "present no objective anomaly of sensation. They can detect, identify and localize pinpricks, and can distinguish quite minor differences in thermal contacts" (ibid., p. 737). The suggestion is that there is actually no loss of pain sensation, but only a loss of typical reactions to painful stimuli: "Experimental interventions which might be expected to give rise to pain provoke neither a verbal protest nor mimic responses, such as wincing, nor yet any vegetative reflex activity" (ibid.). As only pain reactions are, according to Critchley, absent in the syndrome that he is considering, he is recommending that it should be treated as the syndrome of congenital indifference to pain. This is how he describes the distinctive marks of that syndrome:

The most remarkable feature in this syndrome is a typical lack of conformity between the feeling of pain as a discriminative quality of sensation, and the registration of distress, either overtly or automatically. Thus we have a dissociation between the various components of a normal pain-experience, i.e., (1) the qualifying notion of pressure, cutting, heat, etc., which constitutes the nature of pain; (2) the highly unpleasant sensation which constitutes the specific sense-datum of pain; and (3) the feeling tone of displeasure. The first component is cognitive in nature, while the second and third are affective. In cases of congenital indifference to pain the first component is intact, while the third is in abeyance, and perhaps also the second. This discrepancy is reminiscent of what may follow the operation of lobotomy, and also the pain asymbolic of Schilder and Stengel; it differs from these conditions, however, in that they also entail a defect of the second component, i.e., the specific pain-feeling. This component may or may not be intact in cases of congenital indifference to pain. (Ibid., p. 742)

For Critchley, the fact that subjects can readily, upon being noxiously stimulated, feel a pinprick and distinguish between sharp and dull, is taken as a reliable and conclusive sign that they feel pain. He assumes that the sensation of pain has been evoked by the noxious stimulus. As patients are carefree and display no pain reactions, their indifference is interpreted as indifference to pain. Of course, if we are to speak at all about indifference to something, the object of the indifference has to be recognized and distinguished from other objects. But, as I have already pointed out, the stimulus—a pinprick—can be detected and felt as intensely sharp, and yet not be felt as pain or as a sensation which falls under the modality of pain. Because this is true of congenital analgesia, this clinical label should be reserved for description and diagnosis of the relevant syndrome, and not the inappropriate and misleading label of "congenital indifference to pain."

As has been shown, the confusion between indifference to noxious stimulation and indifference to pain basically arises because no clear distinction is made between two distinct sensory capacities: the ability to feel the noxious stimulus—the pinprick—and the ability to feel the sensation of pain. The obliteration of this fundamental distinction has also led some authors to improperly treat cases of indifference to noxious stimulation as cases of pain asymbolia, or as cases of genuine indifference to pain. I have already mentioned the case of the patient with a right parietal and insular lesion, whose ailment was incorrectly diagnosed as pain asymbolia. Recall that the patient studied by Masson et al. (1991, pp. 668–670) did not seem to mind and did not display any reactions to noxious stimuli applied to his right hand. He was mistakenly diagnosed with pain asymbolia simply because he was able to feel a pinprick and distinguish between sharp and dull. If this patient displayed indifference, which he did, it was an indifference to noxious stimulation, not an indifference to pain. The same misunderstanding and misuse of words is found in the case of two patients studied by Rubins and Friedman and treated as paradigm cases of pain asymbolia or indifference to the sensation of pain:

The predominant feature shown by our patients was the pain asymbolia, as described by Schilder. . . . Two patients stated repeatedly that the pinprick didn't hurt even after prolonged application and to the point of drawing blood. . . . Other stimuli such as heat or cold produced a similar result. One patient would hold a lighted match until her fingers would almost burn without dropping it. (Rubins and Friedman 1948, p. 565)

These are, indeed, frightening examples of complete indifference or total absence of reactions to extremely noxious stimuli. But the question is whether these two patients felt pain when they were exposed to such stimuli. Here is how Rubins and Friedman evaluated the sensation of pain and sensibility in other modalities:

Except for the asymbolia, the other modalities of superficial and deep sensation showed little disturbance. Touch and thermal stimulation were well-perceived and to the same extent throughout the body. Passive movement of joints and position of digits in space were normally recognized.

Pain sensation as evaluated by our routine criteria—namely, ability to distinguish between sharp and dull on application of a pointed object or to perceive sharpness with the same intensity—was normal. Subject to the same fluctuation, pinprick was felt as equally sharp wherever applied and distinguished from a blunt stimulus. (Ibid., p. 566)

As Roger Trigg has observed, the problem with Rubins and Friedman's evaluation of pain sensation is that they "do not see the distinction between being able to feel a pinprick and being able to feel sensation with 'pain quality'" (Trigg 1970, p. 73). Elaborating further this basic distinction, Trigg comes to the following conclusion:

If a patient is not numb they (Rubins and Friedman) assume that he can feel pain, and all interest must then center on the patient's ability, or lack of it, to react normally to pain. . . . It is in no way self-contradictory to report sensations of sharpness normally, and yet to deny pain. Just because such sensations may normally possess the quality of pain, it does not follow that they must always. Rubins and Friedman can be accused of paying too much attention to the nature of the stimulus, and not enough to the nature of sensation, as described by the patient. Because a stimulus, such as severe pinprick, is normally painful, they assume that all that is required for the occurrence of pain is that the patient perceive the stimulus. They forget that it is possible for the sensations produced by the same stimulus to vary. (Ibid., pp. 73–74)

The confusion between indifference to noxious stimulation and indifference to pain is also evident in the study conducted by Weinstein, Kahn, and Slote on a group of patients "who appeared inattentive to disabled parts and sides of the body, were mute, hypokinetic, and who showed the phenomenon of pain asymbolia. It was considered that these forms of behavior were in some degree forms of implicit denial of illness" (Weinstein, Kahn, and Slote 1955, p. 235). That pain asymbolia and, consequently, indifference to pain, are incorrectly attributed to these patients becomes clear from the way in which Weinstein, Kahn, and Slote describe the general condition of pain asymbolia allegedly present in 15 out of 20 patients that they examined:

When stimulated vigorously with the point of the pin or in some other noxious fashion, they did not react to the stimulus as though it was painful or unpleasant. Usually, they did not pull away, attempt to brush aside the pin, cry out, wince, or grimace. Similarly they did not heed threatening gestures. Even on the occasion when a patient may act as if a stimulus was painful, on being questioned, he would deny that it hurt. . . . It was not simply a matter of impaired sensation, because many times the patient could distinguish sharp and dull and hot and cold and would complain of pain in another context. (Ibid., p. 240)

The description of a particular patient diagnosed with pain asymbolia fits the general pattern described above:

Vibratory, proprioceptive, and tactile sensibility was normal. The patient was able to distinguish heat from cold and sharp from dull in routine fashion but showed marked pain asymbolia. When stimulated forcibly with a point of a pin or with very hot objects, he gave no indication of feeling pain. Pressure over the Achilles and elbow tendons gave the same result.

The pain asymbolia persisted throughout his hospital stay of a month and for six weeks following discharge. Even though pricked on the point of drawing blood, the patient gave no evidence of perceiving pain. On one occasion a very hot stimulus produced a slight burn. When asked about this on the following day, the patient denied that the examiner had burned him, even though a mark was still present. He confabulated that another doctor who looked like the examiner had accidentally dropped a cigarette ash on him. On another occasion he cut himself shaving but denied both the cut and any pain. The patient presented an overly polite, servile manner. He invariably answered with "Sir," and even called his wife "Ma'am." He always smiled when anyone else smiled. (Ibid., p. 243)

But why attribute pain asymbolia to this patient, when the case report explicitly states that the patient gave no evidence of perceiving pain? The distinctive mark of pain asymbolia is the fact that patients are able to perceive or feel pain, but that it does not bother them. When they are aware of their plight, they do not confabulate. Rather, they try to rationalize their behavior or are simply astonished by it. They tend to underrate the intensity of their pain and they smile or laugh, but only during pain testing, and not when anyone else smiles. They smile at the very pain that they feel or perceive, because they feel or perceive it as a mock threat or false alarm. We must remember that the lobotomy patient observed by Paul Brand also smiled at her pain, because it was no longer the source of great suffering and was no longer a threat for her: "She smiled sweetly and chuckled to herself. 'In fact, it's still agonizing. But I don't mind'" (Brand 1997, p. 210).

The case of the patient studied by Weinstein, Kahn, and Slote should, as far as his loss of pain reactions is concerned, actually be treated as a case of indifference to noxious or harmful stimulation, and not indifference to pain. The very meaning of the word "indifference" implies that the patient is aware of the stimuli as pain; otherwise, it would not be indifference, obliviousness, or insensibility to such stimuli. So, the fact that the patient was able to distinguish between sharp and dull and between hot and cold fits with this description. On the other hand, as the very word "asymbolia" suggests, patients who suffer from pain asymbolia are not able to attach proper meaning or significance to the pain that they literally feel. If they were not feeling or perceiving pain, upon being noxiously stimulated, there would be nothing to which they would fail to attach proper meaning or significance, or smile or laugh at. The very application of the term "pain asymbolia" would not make sense, and in the case of the patient studied by Weinstein, Kahn, and Slote, it does not make sense. The fact that there are conspicuous behavioral differences between this patient and the patients who really suffer from pain asymbolia is important, because it shows that there are observable differences between indifference to noxious stimulation and indifference to pain. In other words, it cannot be objected that the distinction between these two indifferences makes no observational difference and should, thus, be discounted or ignored. Although in both cases pain reactions are absent, the absence or presence of pain or pain sensation is, indeed, the difference that makes a difference to the patient's behavior. It is an anomaly that makes one smile or laugh; that makes one astonished by one's own smiling or laughter; and, finally, that makes one seek an explanation through rationalization rather than confabulation.

Drawing a clear distinction between indifference to pain and indifference to noxious stimuli is also important for the precise description, diagnosis, and explanation of the loss of pain reactions. The loss of normal pain behavior is symptomatic of several psychiatric conditions, including severe depression and catatonic schizophrenia of the self-mutilating subtype. In this context, the study of Hall and Stride is of special interest, because they carefully examined the sensation threshold, the pain threshold, and the pain tolerance threshold in 256 neurotic and depressive patients of both sexes and various ages. Their measurements showed that, in general, "patients classified as depressed tend to have a high pain tolerance. . . . Over 80% of those patients who did not report pain, and of those who did not react to pain, fall into this category" (Hall and Stride 1954, p. 52).

But Hall and Stride noticed that there are two different ways in which depressed patients display high pain tolerance:

In one patient, described clinically as a recurrent endogenous depression, even the perception of warmth occurred beyond the mean point of pain perception for the total group. Verbal report of pain did not occur at all, the intensity of the stimulus at maximum being described as merely warm. The depression here seems to have, at least temporarily, reduced the verbal-perceptual and, perhaps consequently, the motor response system to an inert state in which stimuli are not adequately discriminated. Another kind of high pain threshold is sometimes found in several of the patients classified as involutional-type depressions. . . . One patient in this category did not report pain even at the maximum intensity, but, on being asked to describe the nature of the sensation, he said: "Well, it was like a lighted cigarette end being held against my forehead." This type of patients will frequently describe a sensation as "burning" or "very hot," without, however, making any admission that it was at all what they meant by pain. There is probably very little, if any, difference in perceptual discrimination in these patients from that of other patients or normals. They do, however, differ markedly in their attitude toward the stimulus, in their evaluation as painful or not painful. This is demonstrated also by the fact that these patients report the stimulus as perceptibly warm as early in the scale as most patients of similar age. (Ibid.)

In the case of the patient suffering from endogenous depression, the evidence, as far as the feeling or perception of pain is concerned, is clear and unequivocal. This patient did not feel any pain even at the maximum intensity of the thermal stimulus; and although the patient was able to detect the heat-stimulus at its maximal intensity, owing to the patient's extremely lowered sensitivity, the nature of the stimulus was incorrectly perceived as merely warm. The patient suffering from involutional or agitative depression was, on the contrary, quite capable of adequately perceiving or discriminating the heat stimulus as burning or very hot. Furthermore, his sensitivity was normal because he reported the stimulus as perceptibly warm as early in the scale as anyone would. The only question is whether he felt pain but was not reacting to it emotionally, or whether he is not feeling pain at all. The patient's explicit reports would suggest that he did not feel or perceive pain at the maximally intense heat stimulus, although he was able to recognize the stimulus as burning or very hot. Moreover, the patient denied that by "burning" or "very hot" he meant pain. However, Hall and Stride insist that there is little, if any, difference "in perceptual discrimination in these patients from that of other patients or normals" (ibid.). This implies that the patient is feeling the same kind of sensation as normal people and that only the emotional reaction is absent. In other words, the difference from normal people is simply that severely depressed patients "differ markedly in their attitude towards the stimulus, in their evaluation of it as painful or not painful" (ibid.). But, as Roger Trigg has remarked, the major question is not about the stimulus, but about the sensations caused by the stimulus, and the phrase "evaluation of it as painful" is, in this context, ambiguous:

As Hall and Stride emphasize that these patients have the same feelings as others . . . "painful" is presumably not intended to refer to quality of a sensation, but is used as a synonym for "distressing" or some such word. The claim is, therefore, that these patients are feeling the same kind of sensation as normal people but do not have any emotional reaction. . . . The authors' use of "painful" to mean "distressful" may be usual when what is described as "painful" is a situation, but in connection with sensations "painful" is used to refer to a pain-quality—even if it may carry the idea that we are distressed by it. What they are doing is to define pain as a "sensation that is disliked," and this has the result that they ignore their patient's inability to feel the distinctive quality of pain. (Trigg 1970, p. 69)

If Hall and Stride had spoken of the indifference to noxious or harmful stimulation, all ambiguities, misunderstandings and, most importantly, wrong descriptions of the facts, could have been avoided. At one point, they speak of "indifference to pain stimulation," but this terminology is also misleading because it suggests that the stimulation evokes a pain sensation to which the patient is indifferent. So again, the term "indifference to noxious stimulation" would have averted a lot of misunderstanding.

Keeping in mind the distinction between the two indifferences—one to noxious stimulation and the other to pain—may also help us comprehend the absence of pain reactions

in patients with catatonic schizophrenia, which frequently includes a tendency toward self-mutilation or auto-aggressiveness:

These patients often hurt or mutilate themselves without showing the
slightest apparent sign of pain. Bender and Schilder divided these reactions into two types, according to the dominant mental symptoms of
patients they studied. Those with stupor but without marked tension
showed no reaction whatsoever to pinching, pinprick, or blows but
rapidly and vigorously withdrew on faradic stimulation. Patients with
pronounced "tensions" frequently reacted to prolonged application of
painful stimuli—i.e., pinching or electric shock—but in an inadequate
and local way. For instance, there might be squirming or athetoid movements of the fingers, sometimes spreading up to the arm, occasionally
accompanied with change in respiratory rate with tears in the eyes or
with stiffening of the body. The response is rather a postural attitude
than an action of escape or defense. One of our patients, a man with
catatonia, would role his head from side to side whenever he was
painfully stimulated but never withdrew his limbs. This perverted reaction disappeared when his catatonic state cleared up. (Rubins and
Friedman 1948, p. 555)

Rubins and Friedman appear quite certain of their claim that
the patients described above do not feel pain and, at best, react
to noxious stimuli in an inadequate and local way. The only
exception to the rule—the brisk and vigorous withdrawal on
faradic stimulation—may be attributed to gross, involuntary
muscle contraction. Yet Rubins and Friedman are inclined to
compare schizophrenic patients to pain asymbolics, as described
by Schilder and Stengel.

In order to see whether this comparison is apt, let us look at
the case of a catatonic schizophrenic patient studied by Trelles.
This patient was diagnosed as pain asymbolic because of his
catatonic episodes and especially because of his frequent acts
of self-mutilation, which were not accompanied by any sign of
pain or suffering. For instance, the patient would frequently

burn his hands with cigarettes and would deny any pain; he would punch himself vigorously without feeling any pain and would say that he had done that in order to reassure himself " 'that he is not afraid of pain and that he is brave' " (Trelles 1978, p. 6). Neurological examinations of this patient showed him to be able to distinguish different types of stimulations used for the exploration of superficial sensitivity: tactile, thermal, and painful. However, he would never show suffering, pain, or reactions of defense. When thermal stimulation was applied—very hot water—or sometimes a profound prick with a syringe, he said that it hurt, but he neither withdrew his hand nor displayed any reactions of escape:

The patient is not disturbed that stimulations are incessantly repeated, each time more strongly (pinpricks), and has no intention of protecting himself; the patient obviously knows that these stimulations produce pain and suffering and says: "I know doctor that this hurts, that this pricks and produces pains. . . . How could it not hurt? . . . Someone would suffer . . . but I don't feel. . . ." (Ibid., p. 7)

In this passage, Trelles is wondering whether this patient should be considered as a case of true pain asymbolia. The patient does not feel pain nor does he display reactions to pain during self-mutilation, so it seems that on such occasions he is indifferent to noxious stimuli rather than to pain. However, Trelles is fairly convinced that in the experimental setting, the patient feels or perceives pain upon being noxiously stimulated, because he regularly and reliably perceives the pinprick, pinch, or very hot or very cold stimuli. But is this sufficient evidence to attribute the sensation of pain to a person with a profound lack of pain behavior? The patient knew that these stimuli hurt, and realized someone else would suffer in his position. However, of himself he said: "but I don't feel. . . ." Unfortunately, we are not told *what* the patient does not feel. My guess is: pain.

Now that I have drawn and illustrated the difference between indifference to noxious stimulation and indifference to pain, let us consider in more detail the differences between various species of indifference to pain. As I said, these differences may relate to the scope of the indifference; to its object, and to whether pain is experienced as unpleasant. In order to illustrate these differences, we will consider at some length the indifference to pain of lobotomy recipients, and I will argue that, unlike the indifference of a pain asymbolic, the indifference of lobotomized patients is of limited scope. It is not directed at the very sensation of pain, but rather at its significance, and it need not mean that pain is no longer experienced as unpleasant.

Recall that the prefrontal lobotomy (or leucotomy) is an operation to cut the nerve fibers which connect the frontal lobes to the rest of the brain.

Prefrontal lobotomy, either unilateral or bilateral, is performed by transecting the cerebrum in a plane identified by the coronal suture and the sphenoidal ridge and just anterior to the lateral ventricle. It is estimated that Brodman areas 8, 9, 10, 11, 32, 46 and 47 are isolated by these procedures. (Hardy, Wolff, and Goodel 1952, p. 307)

The operation was widely used in the 1930s, '40s, and '50s to relieve chronic pain of functional or organic origin, and intractable pain in fatal diseases (quite often after a patient had become addicted to "pain-killing drugs"). Surgeons eventually became reluctant to perform the operation because severing the frontal regions from the rest of the brain turned out to have far-reaching effects on personality.

Let us now examine some of the case histories of lobotomy patients as they are presented in Freeman and Watts' famous book, *Psychosurgery in the Treatment of Mental Disorders and Intractable Pain*:

Case 9

A woman of hysterical temperament began at the age of 16 to complain of abdominal pain so persistently that she accumulated a series of 12 to 18 abdominal operations. . . . Following a trivial head injury, she complained so bitterly of pain in the head that a subtemporal decompression was performed. From 1934 to 1936 she was confined to bed because of agonizing pain in the back and limbs. . . . On account of exaggeration of complaints with very little anatomic substrate, a diagnosis of conversion hysteria with poly-surgical addiction was made.

Prefrontal lobotomy was performed November 30, 1936, by the Moniz technique. The change brought about in this patient's fear reaction was immediate and remarkable. On the second postoperative day the patient was alert and fairly talkative and admitted that the sensitiveness that she had formerly felt over the spine has disappeared. . . . The patient turned over on her back, gingerly at first, then with greater confidence. When her lower limbs were manipulated and forced into extension for the first time in many months, there was much crepitation. The patient cried out with pain, but nevertheless seemed to enjoy having her legs straightened out once more.

When the patient returned to the neurology clinic for follow up visits, she appeared to be in good spirits and reported that she felt fine. However, when we asked her specifically about her back, she said: "This back of mine hurts so I can hardly walk." We could find no muscle spasm or rigidity in the spine, although twisting about in various directions brought tears to her eyes and she complained bitterly of pain. After the examination, she dressed herself and walked without showing any evidence of pain.

Comment: When Mrs. S. first told us she had pain six months after operation we feared a relapse. Then it gradually dawned upon us, as we observed this patient's behavior, that she still had pain but was no longer disabled with it; she was not afraid of it, and she could work and earn a living in spite of it. (Freeman and Watts 1950, pp. 354–357)

Case 301

Age 55. Hypochondriasis. Pain in back since girlhood, worse since birth of first child 28 years ago, and unbearable for last three years. . . .

Prefrontal lobotomy of the standard type, performed on March 1, 1945, was followed by alleviation of back pain. . . . By April, 1947, the patient . . . had resumed many of her household activities. She says the pain is still there, but it does not bother her. (Ibid., p. 358)

Case 165

Age 62. Hypochondriasis. Disabling pain since 1931, especially in back and hip. The patient suffered a series of financial reverses after the stock market crashed, and in 1931 developed severe pain in the back and left hip with radiation down the leg. There was also pain across the chest in the region of his heart. . . . A standard prefrontal lobotomy was performed April 14, 1943, after which he stopped complaining about his back and sedation was discontinued. He lives a quiet existence at home and mentions his pains only when asked about them. (Ibid., pp. 358–359)

Case 280

Tabes dorsalis. Ten years' disability with girdle pain and lightning pain in legs. . . . A standard prefrontal lobotomy was performed on December 4, 1944, after which narcotics were discontinued. He continued to have attacks but described them as twinges which he was able to control with aspirin. . . . The neurologic signs of tabes are as obvious as ever. His perception of pain is as keen as before, but his reaction to pain lacks the emotional component that was disabling. (Ibid., pp. 366–367)

The fear of pain in the patients described in this chapter has been the outstanding and disabling feature. After prefrontal lobotomy, these patients can apparently feel pain just as acutely, but they are no longer afraid of pain, nor concerned over the possible consequences. Their perception of pain is intact but their reaction to pain is brief and reduced in intensity. The emotional component is attenuated and the fear of pain is no longer disabling. (Ibid., p. 360)

With respect to the cases of pain of organic origin, Freeman and Watts observed:

preoccupation with pain dominated the life of the individual to the extent that he could no longer carry on his ordinary activities. At the same time, however, he could often be distracted by interesting events in his vicinity and would not mention his distress. . . . There is less obvious relationship in these cases between pain and the emotional status, but the affective charge is highly important. When it is reduced by lobotomy, the pain may become tolerable, opiates can be discontinued . . . and the individual may return to work. (Ibid., p. 360)

Freeman and Watts summarize their general impression of the effects of lobotomy in this way: "The attitude was different. Fear seemed to have gone. The pain was still present, but it was a sensation rather than a threat" (ibid., p. 353); and they continue: "Lobotomy does not interfere with the perception of pain, nor does it abolish the normal reaction to pain. It does reduce the persistent, obsessive, emotional substrate of continued pain. We would compare this situation with the dynamite charge that is detonated by a percussion cup. The emotional substrate represents the explosive, and when this is removed, the percussion cup can go off any number of times without resulting in a great explosion. Case 280, the tabetic, spoke of his twinges" (ibid., p. 372).

However, the case histories presented by Freeman and Watts do not reveal the very important data concerning the intensity of pain before and after the operation of prefrontal lobotomy, nor do they disclose any facts related to the pain sensation threshold and reaction threshold of the patients, either pre- or postoperatively. For this kind of information, we must turn to a study conducted by Hardy, Wolff, and Goodel on a series of 38 prefrontal lobotomies performed by Dr. Bronson Ray in a New York hospital, on patients with intractable pain. These authors report that "in 21 out of 38 persons, following lobotomy, some relief of pain appeared to have been achieved in some way; of these, 17 admitted experiencing pain only when asked; four had no pain at all" (Hardy, Wolff, and Goodel 1952, p. 310).

Measurement of the pain threshold, by the use of the thermal radiation method, was carried out on eight patients before the operation:

The average of all these measurements was 206 mc./sec./cm.2. . . . This is a mean value within the normal range. . . . Pain threshold measurements were made in ten patients post-operatively. In two patients the pain threshold was observed to be lowered immediately following operation. In one of these who was observed again two weeks post-operatively the pain threshold had returned to the pre-operative level. In three patients who had been measured pre-operatively the post-operative pain threshold was unaltered. In five patients who were not measured pre-operatively, measurements one week or more post-operatively gave pain thresholds within the normal range, 200 to 230 mc./sec./cm. 2. The mean of all post-operative pain thresholds measurements was 209 mc./sec./cm2, a value which is not significantly different from the pre-operative level. (Ibid., p. 322)

These results led Hardy, Wolff, and Goodel to the general conclusion that "although the pain threshold may show temporary alterations, the average of the pain threshold before and after operation is essentially the same" (ibid.).

The measurements of pain intensity in five patients before and after the operation showed that the preoperative pain was, in general, "of low intensity with brief episodes of more intense pain accompanying a disturbance of a diseased part. However, at no time was any patient completely free of pain. These two factors characterized the pain picture in these patients" (ibid., p. 313). As far as the postoperative data on pain intensity are concerned, it turned out that for only one patient the intractable pain was completely eliminated, while for the other four, "the pain was reduced on the average and in maximum value. However, they were at no time pain free" (ibid.). An examination of the postoperative reaction thresholds of 23 lobotomized patients—that is, the wincing and pulling of their heads in response to thermal radiation—also showed that there is no major alteration in reaction to new or fresh or short-lived noxious stimulation, and/or that the reaction can sometimes be more vigorous than before the operation (Chapman, Solomon, and Rose 1950, pp. 386–392). This is in accord with the bedside observation that, "when suddenly moved or turned over, the patient, who until this time may have been relaxed and tranquilly resting in bed, may cry out vigorously with pain from bombardment of additional noxious impulses from his damaged bone or joint structure" (Hardy, Wolff, and Goodel 1952, p. 320).

When these results of the measurements of pain intensity, pain sensation, and pain reaction thresholds in lobotomized patients are taken into account, it seems that the major effects of the operation are not changes in pain perception, intensity discriminations, or reactions to momentary harmful stimuli. According to Hardy, Wolff, and Goodel, the most important changes are observed in the patients' affect and attitude toward pain: "The lobotomized subjects became indifferent to low intensity pain which, though perceived, evoked few protective reactions. The attitude was epitomized in the response, 'Yes, I feel the pain, but it doesn't bother me'" (ibid., p. 316).

[These subjects also] exhibited a freedom from anxiety about pain, did not anticipate its occurrence and lacked an interest in recall and description of pain experienced in the past. Each painful experience was dealt with in its own terms as a fresh experience. They showed little concern about the implications of pain as regards damage to the body or threat to life. . . . Indeed, these subjects exhibited in many ways, notably concerning the topic of pain, a flattened affect if not actual apathy. When noxious stimulation of high intensity was suddenly imposed upon them experimentally or by some surgical procedure, despite immediate vigorous reactions, these subjects promptly ceased to exhibit evidence of pain, "forgot" their recent experiences, and turned to the casual reading of a newspaper or idly looking about. (Ibid., pp. 316–317)

The following profile is typical of lobotomized patients: "lack of complaint and failure to call attention to their plight and needs were striking. They failed not only to complain of their spontaneous pain but also of their needs, such as personal nursing care, need of urine bottle, bedpan, or the adjustment of uncomfortable dressing. When incontinent of feces they were indifferent to odor. It spread about their persons and beds" (ibid.).

Although the operation of prefrontal lobotomy for intractable pain has no uniform effects, there are still some standard or definite patterns of reactions characteristic of all lobotomized patients. The first trend that emerges is the fact that such patients, though not minding the pain of their disease, feel and dislike other transient pains. The measurement of their pain sensation and pain reaction thresholds supports this observation, which is very important because it shows that lobotomized patients are using the concept of pain properly, that is, under standard stimulation conditions followed by typical pain behavior. In other words, it cannot be claimed that these subjects are confused about or that they have even forgotten the very meaning of the word "pain."

The second characteristic feature is the radical change in their readiness to complain of pain. Before the operation, the pain absorbed their whole attention—they were obsessed by it—but after the operation, they tended to speak about their pain and complain of it only when explicitly questioned. This seems to be related to the fact that their concern became narrowed down to the immediate present—that they would see and care little for anything outside the actual present.

The third behavioral pattern characteristic of postlobotomy patients can be described, in general terms, as a "mitigated 'readiness to respond' to external and internal stimuli" (Barber 1959, p. 439). This decreased responsiveness is probably caused by a change in personality and is manifested in its extreme form in total apathy, and in its lesser forms in a decrease in worry and concern or in ability to elaborate a persisting attitude or mood.

The three behavioral patterns presented above seem to show that in lobotomized patients, the sensation of pain remains, but the dread, anxiety, or fear that formerly accompanied pain has disappeared. They worry about it little or not at all, although any sudden change in their pain, or any new pain, is liable to evoke an immediate (but fleeting) response. Does this mean that for postlobotomy patients, their permanent but disregarded pain is no longer the object of dislike? In other words, has their pain ceased to be unpleasant for them?

If an answer to these questions is to be given, we have to draw a distinction between two kinds of emotional reactions to pain, a distinction which is not always made clear in discussions of this topic. On the one hand, there are emotional reactions which take the very sensation of pain as their object and depend upon its quality, intensity, location, and duration. On the other hand, there are emotional reactions which are directed at the *significance* or meaning of the pain, and which depend primarily upon the meaning that we attach to the pain that we feel. Dislike, a feeling of unpleasantness, or distress belong to the first category of emotional reactions to pain, while anxiety, dread, or fear are to be reckoned among the second category. Although these two kinds of emotional reactions to pain usually occur together, changes in emotional reaction of the second kind do not necessarily bring about changes in emotional reactions of the first kind. In other words, the anxiety, fear, or dread related to the meaning of the pain that we currently feel may subside, while the unpleasantness or distress that we feel over it might well persist. For instance, I am suffering from glaucoma, which was, fortunately, diagnosed in its early stage and is under medical control. Still, if I were to feel a sharp, intense pain in my eyes, I would become frightened, because I know that this kind of pain may be a sign of the deteriorating state of my eyes. My fear would alarm me, and I would certainly visit my oph-thalmologist. If he reassured me that there was nothing wrong with my intraocular pressure and that there had been no change in my visual field, my fear would subside. But the pain could still be unpleasant or distressing, even though I would no longer be worried about it and would find a way to live with it.

The major effect of the operation of prefrontal lobotomy is, then, the disappearance of the anxiety, fear, or dread that the patients formerly felt about their sustained, intractable pain. Again, as Freeman and Watts put it: "The attitude was different. The pain was still present, but it was a sensation rather than a threat" (1950, p. 353). This change in the attitude of loboto-mized patients toward their pain seems to be the outcome of a more general change in their emotional setup, reflected in their "flattened affect" and the fact that their concern has narrowed down to the immediate present. Because they do not attach to their permanently present pain the meaning or significance that they ascribed to it before the operation, it does not bother them or they do not mind it anymore. But it does not follow that they do not dislike it anymore, or that it has ceased to be unpleasant for them. As we have seen, one may not be bothered by something or not mind it anymore, once it has been robbed of its former significance, although the unpleasantness itself may remain unchanged. Of course, this will depend very much on the intensity of pain; but, as we have seen in the case of lobotomized patients, their pain was mostly—though sustained—of moderate intensity. Where it was severe, one might explain their not being bothered by it or not minding it by the fact that they had been reduced to a state of total apathy.

Generally speaking, the clinical, psychological, and behavioral profile of the lobotomized patients does not lend support to the view that, for them, pain is no longer unpleasant or that it has stopped being the object of their dislike. If that is true, it means that we are not compelled to give up our well-entrenched intuition that pain is inherently unpleasant on the account of the reports of lobotomized patients who claim that they still feel pain, but that it does not bother them anymore or that they do not mind or dislike it anymore. In other words, indifference to pain need not mean that the ongoing pain is no longer disliked or no longer felt as unpleasant; it may only mean—as the case of lobotomy patients shows—that one does not care or mind it because it is no longer the object of anxiety, fear, depression, or frustration related to its past or its long-term future implications. Let me remind you once again that the patient observed by Paul Brand still described her pain as agonizing, but also as something that she no longer minded:

As a German neurosurgeon who had performed many prefrontal lobotomies once told me, "The procedure takes all the suffering out of pain." Stages one and two of pain, the signal and message stages, proceed without interruption. But a radical change in stage three, the mind's response, transforms the nature of the overall experience. (Brand and Yancey 1997, p. 211)

In lobotomy patients, indifference to persistent pain is the consequence of their inability to ascribe any lasting or long-term significance to the ongoing chronic pain: "Subjects with prefrontal lobotomies or leukectomies have severe disruption of their abilities to cognitively assess the meaning and implications of chronic pain. However, these subjects have normal or even lowered pain thresholds and retain their ability to experience both sensory and early affective components of pain" (Coghill et al. 1999, p. 1941). Wade et al. speak of the first stage of pain affect (or pain unpleasantness) and the second stage of pain affect as having to do with emotions related to the long-term implications of pain. They claim that

nearly all of the affective verbal descriptors of the McGill Pain Questionnaire refer much more to the immediate threat and unpleasantness . . . of pain. . . . For example, the words "tiring," "exhausting," "sickening," and "suffocating" refer to unpleasant intrusive aspects of pain closely associated with sensory qualities and words such as "fearful," "frightening," or "terrifying" refer to the immediate threat associated with pain. In contrast, answers to questions about how depressed, anxious, and frustrated one feels in relation to one's pain rely more on reflection concerning the past and long-term future implications of a persistent pain condition. (Wade et al. 1996, pp. 163–164)

That lobotomized patients are, indeed, able to experience both the sensory and the early affective components of pain has already been well established. So, an additional piece of evidence will be presented just to give us better insight into the real scope, proper object, and genuine character of the indifference to pain displayed by these patients: It should be emphasized that the lobotomized patient is able to respond normally to noxious stimulation. Hardy, Wolff, and Goodel (1952, p. 316) have reported that "some patients, although ostensibly tranquil before being asked about their pain, overreacted with a show of grimacing and fears when their attention was focused upon it by a direct question concerning its quality and its intensity":

Apparently, when the leucotomized patient is directly asked to report on his pain, he "focuses his attention" on and "thinks about" the ever-present nociceptive stimulus in his body and, when thus reacting to it, often shows discomfort and suffering and almost always reports a "sensation of pain." However, when the patient is not directly asked to report on his condition, he does not "attend" to it or "think" about it to the same extent as before the operation and, when not thus reacting to it, does not appear to be "in pain." (Barber 1959, p. 439)

Taking this additional piece of evidence into account, along with the other evidence at hand, it is obvious that the indifference to pain displayed by lobotomy patients is strictly limited to ongoing or persistent pain; that its object is not the very sensation of pain, but its lasting meaning or significance; and that this kind of indifference does not imply that pain is no longer disliked or experienced as unpleasant. Indifference to pain of this limited scope and character is fundamentally the consequence of the more general deficit or incapacity of lobotomy patients to pay close attention and give lasting meaning to any novel, threatening, discomforting, or disgusting stimuli.

Indifference to ongoing persistent pain is also characteristic of patients who have undergone cingulotomy for the relief of chronic intractable pain. After this kind of psychosurgery, cingulotomized patients, like lobotomized patients, admit that they still have pain, but say that it is not distressing or bothersome and does not worry them anymore. These patients are similar to lobotomized patients in another respect. They also react vigorously to any newly inflicted pain:

Numerous clinical studies report decreases in the suffering, distress, and analgesic requirements that follow frontal leucotomies and cingulotomies for the treatment of the intractable chronic pain. Many of these same studies, however, also document a persistence after neurosurgical lesions of exaggerated withdrawal responses, wincing, and grimacing, which are evoked by even trivial clinical procedures such as pinprick and venipuncture. (Talbot et al. 1995, p. 124)

Paradoxically, the relief of pain and suffering is achieved despite exaggerated behavioral responses to noxious stimulation. This only proves that indifference to pain is of limited scope in both lobotomized and cingulotomized patients. Unlike lobotomy, cingulotomy does not have serious effects on the personality of the patient and does not seriously impair his cognitive capacities. However, a recent study of 18 patients has shown that it impairs, to a significant extent, certain faculties of attention and executive control:

Most patients reported mild improvements in pain severity, although none reported a complete absence of pain. Most patients reported overall benefit from cingulotomy and being less bothered by pain.... Cingulotomy patients showed poorer performance than control subjects on tests of ability to focus on and sustain attention to the task at hand, they also showed impairments on attention/executive measures of response intention, generation, and persistence. (Cohen et al. 1999, p. 450)

So it seems that the major effect of cingulotomy is to attenuate the tendency of patients to continuously respond, emotionally and behaviorally, to their ever-present pain, and this squares well with their reports that the pain is still there but is not bothersome or is less bothersome than before. In this respect, like lobotomy patients, cingulotomy patients show reduced spontaneous concern and rumination about their persistent pain; but for both groups of patients, the following is true:

[These patients] can experience the immediate threat of pain once it is brought to their attention. In contrast, asymbolia patients appear incapable of perceiving the threat of nociceptive stimuli under any circumstances. (Price 2000, p. 1771)

In other words, only in the case of pain asymbolia patients do we see total or complete indifference to pain, because only these patients have ceased to care about any kind of pain inflicted anywhere on their bodies, and only these patients no longer experience pain as unpleasant or as something that is disliked per se. One must say that, even in the indifference to pain displayed by morphinized subjects, the unpleasantness of pain still seems to be present. One recent study of the effects of oral morphine on cold pressor tolerance time came to the following conclusion:

Subjects who received oral morphine . . . showed increased pain tolerance time in comparison with the control subjects receiving the active placebo (diphenhydramine). The morphine dose of 0.429 mg/kg produced a significantly longer tolerance than did the active placebo. Although a significant increase in tolerance time in the cold pressor task was observed, there were no significant reductions in either pain intensity or unpleasantness ratings during cold pressor for either the morphine or diphenhydramine groups.

Morphine and diphenhydramine produced similar changes in mood. . . . These mood changes included . . . reductions of anxiety and fearfulness. (Cleeland et al. 1996, p. 260)

In pain asymbolia patients, thorough indifference to pain is due to the fact that these patients are entirely incapable of appreciating the threat and unpleasantness of pain, despite their capacity to perceive its sensory features. Consequently, they are not able to ascribe to their pain any long-term or lasting meaning or significance. But if pain without any painfulness is possible, as the case of asymbolia patients unequivocally shows, should we abandon our deep conviction that pain is inherently unpleasant? Should we revise our concept of pain so that we no

longer assume that pain is inextricably bound to unpleasantness? I think that we should not, for the case of pain asymbolia should instead be viewed as a phenomenon which clearly
shows us what pain comes to when it is deprived of unpleasantness—that is, it reminds us that the bare sensation of pain
comes to nothing and serves no biological purpose. To put this
point in other words and make a final conclusion: the indifference to pain displayed in pain asymbolia patients is so thorough
and complete the patients can do nothing but laugh at it.

8 C-Fibers and All That

When we considered the basic neural mechanisms and structures of the self-protective human pain system, we discussed the important roles of C-and A-Δ nociceptive fibers in pain sensation. Recall that a fair amount is known about these fibers. Their physiological specialization has been precisely determined; the distinctive qualitative character of the pain that their activity typically elicits has been described; and, finally, the motor reactions evoked by their firing have been quite clearly specified.

The strange thing is that C-fibers, of all sensory fibers detected in sensory physiology, are certainly the most popular sensory units among philosophers. For some reason, C-fibers have become celebrities while the unfortunate A-Δ nociceptive fibers have been almost completely ignored in philosophy of mind. Everybody who is familiar with contemporary materialism has heard of C-fibers, because the firing of these units was singled out as the neural (physical) activity with which the experience of pain is to be identified: "pain = C-fiber firing." The reason for this identity, as far as I know, was never clearly stated. Since these fibers were introduced in philosophy as (either referential or functional) identificational targets of pain, data about their distinctive morphological, physiological, and psychological properties have been conspicuously absent. Philosophers almost never mentioned the relevant electrophysiological and psychophysical studies. As Daniel Dennett, one of the few philosophers who does pay attention to the facts of the neural mechanisms of pain, has observed:

During the heated debate between materialists, functionalists, and subjectivists in the sixties and seventies of the last century, the term "C-fiber" or "C-fiber firing" seems to have lost, for philosophers, its empirical anchoring in neuroanatomy and became a philosopher's wildcard referring expression for whatever physical event "turns out to be identical with" pain. (Dennett 1978, p. 450, n. 4)

Some philosophers have "located" these quasi-mythical peripheral afferent fibers in the *brain*(!). Some refer to them as "pain fibers," obliterating the distinction between the physiological and psychological specificity of sensory fibers. Finally, philosophers' C-fibers have been stripped of any sensory-discriminative role in pain experience. The worst is yet to come in the guise of the final philosophical verdict on the poor C-fibers. Van Gulick is bold enough to speak about the discovery of C-fibers firing as "the standard philosophical candidate for the neural basis of pain, despite its total empirical implausibility." The same attitude is found in David Lewis: "So if the state pain is C-firing, to take a toy example, then the distinctive quale of pains would be the property; being an event of C-firing" (1995, p. 141).

One need only remind oneself of the analgesia that leprosy patients suffer from as a result of the destruction of peripheral nociceptors—C-fibers included—to see how these statements or proclamations are unfounded. So, after being uncritically introduced into philosophy, C-fibers have ended up being uncritically rejected. But this is just a case, as will be shown, of philosophical disregard for the relevant facts, and has no bearing on the important theoretical issues related to the connection between the firing of C-fibers and the experience of pain. The important claim, the real challenge, is to be found in Joseph Levine's statement:

There seems to be nothing about C-fiber firing which makes it naturally "fit" the phenomenal properties of pain, any more than it would fit some other set of phenomenal properties. . . . The identification of the qualitative side of pain with C-fiber firing (or some property of C-fiber firing) leaves the connection between it and what we identify it with completely mysterious. One might say it makes the way pain feels into a merely brute fact. (Levine 1983, p. 357)

In order to see whether psychophysical connections are really doomed to remain just a matter of brute, unintelligible correlations, I will discuss at some length the basic physiological properties of C-fibers, and describe the distinctive psychological consequences of their activity. As far as these properties of C-fibers are concerned, two important things have been conclusively established through electrophysiological and psychophysical studies: first, that these fibers—along with A-Δ fibers—selectively or preferentially respond to noxious or potentially noxious stimuli (stimuli which, if prolonged, would damage the tissue); and second, that their activity elicits dull or burning pain, while the firing of A-Δ fibers elicits sharp or pricking pain. So, let us consider how these properties of C and A-Δ fibers were discovered, and whether they can help us to see that there is not only a brute correlation, but also an intelligible connection between the firing of these fibers and pain experience.

C-fibers, like A-Δ fibers, are to be found in all mammals, and are widely distributed in skin as well as in deep tissue. They not only outnumber A-Δ fibers, but also all other sensory fibers, particularly in human beings. Morphologically C-fibers and A-Δ fibers are small-diameter primary afferent neurons: the sensory nerve units which consist, at least, "of a receptive terminal located in peripheral tissue, a peripheral afferent fiber that represents a conductive link, a cell body in a dorsal root or trigeminal ganglion, and central terminals in the spinal cord or medulla" (Perl 1984, p. 25). But C-fibers differ from A-Δ fibers in two important respects. First, they are not covered by cuffs of myelin, a laminated fat-protein insulating material. Second, they transmit nerve impulses more slowly than A-Δ fibers. Their conduction velocity ranges from 0.5 to 1.5 meters per second, while that of A-Δ fibers ranges from 6 to 30 meters per second. So, it can take more than a second for the nerve impulses from an injured foot conducted by C-fibers to reach the spinal cord, while the nerve impulses transmitted by A-Δ fibers from the same part of the body would reach the spinal cord long before.

The physiological specialization of C-fibers and A-Δ fibers, like the specialization of other sensory fibers, has been studied in two ways: first, by dissecting out the nerve and recording its activity under a certain range of natural stimuli with gross (silver) hook electrodes; second, by percutaneously inserting tungsten needle microelectrodes into the nerve in order to record impulses from a single fiber evoked upon delivery of natural stimuli to the skin or deep tissue. The former method was used in animal experiments, while the latter has enabled physiologists to perform electrophysiological experiments in awake human subjects. This invasive electrophysiological technique, known as microneurography, was developed in the late 1960s (Vallbo and Hagbarth 1968). Microneurography revolutionized the field of sensory physiology, because it enabled researchers to record impulses from single sensory units in an intact human subject. In other words, it has largely materialized the desire "to compare both stimulus and sensation with the messages which pass up the sensory nerve fibers" (Adrian 1931, p. 1).

The electrophysiological techniques described above have made it possible to determine the adequate stimulus for sensory fibers: that is, the stimulus to which they best respond. It has been discovered that, among A-Δ and C-fibers, there are fibers which preferentially react to strong mechanical stimuli (like stroking, scratching, or pinpricking), to temperatures above 45°C or below 23°C, and to chemical irritants (e.g., histamine). Although these stimuli are of quite different modes, they have, as Sherrington long ago noticed, "in relation to the organism one feature common to all its components, namely, a nocuous character" (1948, p. 227). That is to say, they are "either frankly tissue damaging or are of such intensity that any small increase or long maintenance of stimulation results in tissue damage" (Price and Dubner 1977, p. 307). This is why stimuli of this kind have been labeled "noxious or *potentially* noxious stimuli," and why the fibers that were discovered to respond preferentially to such stimuli have been classified as nociceptive fibers. The existence of such fibers was anticipated by Sherrington several decades ago (1948, pp. 229–230). Fibers of this type will react to temperatures around 48°C, at which nerve substance begins to suffer injury. These fibers will respond to the pressure of the thorn or needle just below the pressure sufficient to break the skin. Moreover, their firing will activate withdrawal or flexion reflexes, and thus initiate one of the basic protective actions of the organism with respect to the stimuli that are of such intensity as threatens damage to the skin (Melzack and Wall 1988, pp. 102–103).

Among A-Δ fibers, there are fibers which best respond to only one kind of noxious or potentially noxious stimulus. Thus, there are A-Δ fibers which preferentially react to mechanical noxious stimuli, and are consequently labeled A-Δ mechano-nociceptive fibers; there are also fibers which respond mostly to noxious heat stimuli, called A-Δ heat nociceptive fibers; and finally, fibers which were discovered to react best to chemical irritants are classified as A-Δ chemo-nociceptive fibers. C-fibers typically respond to all three noxious or potentially noxious stimuli—mechanical, thermal, and chemical—which is why they are called C-poly-modal nociceptive fibers (Melzack and Wall 1988, pp. 86–87). Recently, new classes of C-fibers have been discovered—the so-called "silent" C-nociceptive-chemo fibers—which do not respond to immediate noxious stimuli, not even to a severe stimulus, but respond to the slow changes in the state of inflamed peripheral tissue. Or they start to react to chemicals released after the injury has been inflicted to joints, muscles, or nerves (McMahon and Koltzenburg 1990). Their activity is usually followed by tenderness (primary and secondary hyper-algesia and hyperesthesia) which spreads around the damaged part of the body, making it extremely sensitive, even to innocuous stimuli. This tenderness strongly discourages movement and manipulation that would disrupt the healing process.

In order to avoid misunderstanding or conceptual confusion, it should be remarked that the classification of a certain group of sensory fibers according to their physiological specialization, or the stimulus to which they best respond, is not meant to imply that they do not react at all to other stimuli, or that other kinds of fibers cannot also react to the stimuli to which the specialized fibers are attuned. The notion of an "adequate stimulus" for receptors and fibers of the sensory system—the notion considered to be a biological principle or law—is only to be understood as the ability of the sensory unit to effectively and reliably distinguish between different stimuli in the impulses it sends to the central nervous system. This conception of the adequate stimulus is clearly stated in Sherrington's original definition of the physiological specialization of sensory receptors and fibers:

The sensorial end-organ is an apparatus by which an afferent nerve fiber is rendered distinctively amenable to some particular physical agent, and at the same time less amenable to, i.e. shielded from, other excitants. It lowers the value of the limen of one particular kind of stimulus, it heightens the value of the limen of stimuli of other kinds. (1900, p. 995)

The merits of this definition of receptor and fiber specialization in terms of the lowest limen (or threshold) for the particular stimulus are twofold: first, it does not exclude the possibility that stimuli other than the one to which the receptor or fiber most sensitive can elicit its activity; second, it allows that other receptors or fibers can react to that stimulus. Thus, in the case that we are interested in, the physiological specialization of the C- and A-Δ fibers as nociceptive sensory units is determined according to the following criterion: "the ability of the sensory unit to effectively and reliably distinguish between noxious and innocuous events in the signals it provides to the central nervous system" (Burgess and Perl 1973, p. 59). There are, indeed, A-Δ mechanical nociceptive fibers which respond only when the stimulus intensity is noxious or nearly noxious (ibid., pp. 62–63); but there are also A-Δ and C-nociceptive fibers which are activated by innocuous thermal and mechanical stimuli. So, what really makes them nociceptive sensory units is the fact that they respond with higher frequency to noxious as opposed to innocuous stimulation of the skin or other tissue, or that they show systematic differences in the discharge patterns for these two stimuli. On the other hand, there are low-threshold mechanoreceptors that are preferentially excited by the nondamaging mechanical disturbances of the skin, but which can also respond to mechanical noxious or potentially noxious stimuli. However, careful studies employing natural stimulus-electrical response methodology have shown that these receptors do not display any systematic differences in the discharge patterns for these two stimuli; and this is to be taken as a proof of the inability of individual mechanoreceptors "to provide appropriate information for distinguishing noxious from innocuous mechanical stimuli" (ibid., pp. 60–61).

In the early 1980s, the technique of human microneurography was supplemented by the method of intraneural microstimulation. This advance has greatly enhanced psychophysical studies whose aim is to relate the activity of single afferent fibers or bundles of such fibers to the sensory judgments concerning the quality, temporal profile, magnitude, and localization of the sensations evoked by that activity. It has been found that the same microelectrode inserted percutaneously into the peripheral nerves of awake subjects, in order to record the afferent discharges of sensory fibers delivered by natural stimuli, can be used to stimulate electrically mechanoreceptive or nociceptive units so as to elicit "elementary sensations" with distinct qualities, temporal characteristics, felt as though originating in a discrete, mono-focal area of the skin (Torebjörk and Ochoa 1980; Ochoa and Torebjörk 1983, 1989; Wall and McMahon 1985; Torebjörk, Vallbo, and Ochoa 1987).

Intraneural microstimulation has made it possible to use a stimulus which selectively activates nociceptive units, by bypassing cutaneous (peripheral) receptors whose activity, induced by natural or electrical stimulation, "unavoidably co-activate[s] unknown numbers of units of imperfectly established physiological identity" (Ochoa and Torebjörk 1989, p. 594). In order to appreciate the technical achievements and research potential of this method, it should be stressed that the distinguished researcher Sinclair made the following statement as recently as the late 1960s:

> To stimulate a single fiber in an intact human subject, to prove satisfactorily that only that fiber and no other has been stimulated, and to record a meaningful sensory judgment is an almost incredibly difficult technical feat, and it will be a long time before unequivocal evidence can be obtained. (Sinclair 1967, p. 12)

Before psychophysical studies using intraneural microstimulation (INMS) can be carried out, the physiological type of the sensory units which are to be examined with regard to the psychological consequences of their electrical stimulation must be identified. The first step is to insert the microelectrode "manually through the skin into an underlying nerve trunk . . . and to deliver trains of weak electrical stimuli while gently adjusting its position," until it has "reached an intrafascicular site where INMS evoked a weak, mono-focally projected sensation" (Ochoa and Torebjörk 1989, p. 585). The area or the site where the sensation evoked by INMS was felt by the subject is denoted as the projected sensory field. When this is established, the electrode is switched to recording mode to determine the receptive field of the sensory unit which has been previously stimulated, that is, the field from which a sensory unit can be activated by natural stimuli. This is done by delivering such stimuli to the cutaneous field where the sensation was projected in order to record intraneurally by microneurography the responses of sensory units. When the unitary receptive field has been localized, its area is outlined with ink on the skin, and the physiological type of the sensory unit whose activity is recorded is identified on the basis of its stimulus-response characteristics, that is, according to the stimuli to which it preferentially responds. A needle electrode is optionally inserted in the receptive field to stimulate the sensory fiber, and its conduction velocity is then "calculated from measurement of latency and conduction distance between stimulating and recording sites" (ibid.). Finally, proof that the fiber stimulated and the fiber recorded are one and the same

can be obtained by "marking" the stimulated fiber: prolonged, high frequency intraneural microstimulation can render that single . . . sensory fiber hyperexcitable. . . . Upon intraneural micro-recording this fiber will either discharge spontaneously or will generate a burst in response to a triggering pulse. Impulses evoked from the receptive field of that particular unit only will now interfere with or trigger activity in the hyperexcitable unit. . . . Thus, it can be certified that a recorded unit with defined receptor characteristics and conduction velocity is identical with the unit stimulated in the nerve. (Torebjörk and Ochoa 1980, p. 445)

The psychophysical studies that we are particularly interested in were carried out on "seventy-one C poly-modal nociceptors supplying glabrous and hairy skin in limbs of awake human volunteers," and their physiological type was identified "on the basis of cutaneous stimulus-response characteristics recorded intraneurally by microneurography" (Ochoa and Torebjörk 1989, p. 583). For this purpose, "natural mechanical stimuli (stroking, scratching, pinpricking), heat (contact of a glowing match) and occasionally histamine (intra-dermal injection . . .) were given to the cutaneous field, where sensations were projected. Having localized the unitary receptive field (RF) and classified the receptor according to established criteria, the receptive field was mapped . . . and its area was outlined with ink on the skin" (ibid., p. 585). C-nociceptors in glabrous skin of the hand were polymodal "in the sense that they all responded to noxious mechanical and heat stimuli. A few units tested also responded to histamine injection and became spontaneously active thereafter. The receptive fields were small, usually 2×2 to 3×3 mm. Conduction velocities ranged from 0.5 to $1.5 \,\mathrm{m\,s^{-1}}$" (ibid., p. 591).

All the units to be tested psychophysically were also "marked" by the standard methods described above. During psychophysical studies,

the subjects had no clues as to exactly when intraneural stimuli were given, or what stimulus parameters were used. . . . They were asked to describe in their own words the qualities and temporal profiles of sensations evoked by INMS, and to map directly on a real size picture of the hand the sites and sizes of the skin areas where sensations were projected. . . . If the subjects had difficulties in naming the sensations, they were presented with a multiple choice questionnaire, composed from typical verbalizations collected in previous studies. (Ibid., p. 586)

Microneurography and INMS were carried out on five healthy subjects, ranging in age from 33 to 51 years. Fourteen experiments were performed in the median nerve at elbow level. . . . Eight experiments were performed in the ulnar nerve, and one experiment in the superficial radial nerve at wrist level. A few experiments used the posterior cutaneous nerve of the forearm . . ., or the perineal nerve at knee level . . ., or just above the ankle. . . . A total of seventy-one C poly-modal nociceptor units with receptive fields in glabrous (thirty-seven units) and hairy (thirty-four units) skin of the hand, forearm, leg or foot were sampled in this study. (Ibid., p. 584)

These studies have shown that pain evoked as threshold sensation during weak INMS delivered in cutaneous nerve fascicles "was regularly projected superficially to the skin. . . . The quality of pain projected to the glabrous skin was often described as dull (thirteen experiments) or less frequently as burning (five experiments). By contrast, pain projected to hairy skin of the dorsum of the hand, forearm or lateral calf was typically reported as burning (all six experiments)" (ibid., p. 589). As reported separately, "the subjective experience of focal pricking or stinging pain was found to correlate with excitation of A nociceptor units" (ibid., p. 587), and such pain is projected to a punctuate area of the skin, whereas the burning or dull pain evoked by the stimulation of C nociceptors is projected to a significantly larger area of the skin.

C-locognosia tests, devised to determine the degree of accuracy to which subjects can locate a painful event in the glabrous skin of the hand based on the input from C-nociceptive fibers alone, have shown "the remarkable matching between the sensory projections (projected field) of dull or burning pain evoked by INMS, and the innervation territories (the receptive field) of C nociceptor fibers alone. . . . It was found that the mean error in localizing a hot stimulus during A fiber block was 7.5 mm in the fingers . . . and 10.5 mm in the palm of the hand" (ibid., p. 593). Thus, it appears

that the C-fiber system can provide useful input for fairly accurate localization of noxious events, at least in the glabrous skin of the hand. . . . It seems obvious that accurate cerebral localization function requires very refined circuitry. . . . Such function appears reserved for pain as a signal of noxious challenge to the body surface which needs to be well localized for the purposes of removal of agent, projection of the injured site or inhibition by gentle rubbing or scratching. (Ibid., p. 597)

As for the temporal profile of the painful sensations evoked by the intraneural microstimulation of C-nociceptive fibers, experiments have shown that both dull and burning pain were sustained sensations, without intermittency:

In other words, subjects could not detect the frequency of intraneural stimulation. At very low (1 Hz) frequency of stimulation usually no sensation was felt during a 5 s train. At 3 Hz gradual build-up of pain was noticed, often following a long latency of the order of 2–3 s relative to the onset of the stimulus train. With higher frequencies (5–30 Hz) the build-up of pain was faster, and the magnitude of pain increased proportionally to the stimulus frequency. (Ibid., p. 589)

This last point shows that the modulation of impulse frequency in a single sensory unit may be enough to signal intensity of a stimulus. Indeed, "firing frequency is translated into intensity of continuous percepts (pressure, pain), but determines the frequency of intermittent percepts (flutter-vibration)" (Torebjörk and Ochoa 1980, p. 447). However, it should be stressed that the sensory modality does not change with frequency. That is, the psychophysical studies, based on the intraneural microstimulation of sensory fibers of different morphological and physiological type, have proved the quantal nature of elementary sensations evoked by the activity of these fibers:

When a sensation first became detectable during intraneural stimulation, it typically remained invariant within a certain current range with regard to quality, temporal profile, subjective magnitude, location, and the size and shape of the projection area. A gradual increase of stimulus intensity above threshold for the first sensation usually lead to discontinuous recruitment of additional sensations with new and discrete projections, rather than to continuous growth of intensity and projection area of the first sensation. New sensations were therefore abruptly recruited at individual stimulation thresholds, according to the all-or-none principle, and each could be characterized by its specific quality, typical temporal profile and spatially distinct projection area. . . . We interpret these quantal changes in the evoked sensory experience as the subjective counterpart to electrophysiological recruitment of separate single sensory units. (Torebjörk, Vallbo, and Ochoa 1987, p. 1522)

It seems to me that the research on the sensory consequences of the intraneural microstimulation of C-nociceptive fibers fully supports the conclusion reached by the authors of these studies:

[There was a] remarkable matching of physiological unit type (C poly-modal nociceptor) with subjective quality of evoked sensation (dull or burning pain). Further, there was remarkable spatial matching of recep-tive field of given C nociceptor with projected field of the pain sensa-tion evoked from the C recording site by INMS delivered at threshold intensity for conscious sensation. (Ochoa and Torebjörk 1989, p. 583)

The evidence that the sensation of pain is closely connected to the firing of nociceptive fibers (both of A-Δ and C type) is, indeed, impressive; but it probably will not impress philoso-phers who are mainly concerned with the "hard" problems of consciousness related to the connection between the firing of C- and A-Δ nociceptive fibers and pain. Of course, they will admit that strong correlations between the activity of certain neural structures and the experience of pain have been estab-lished. They will certainly recognize that these correlations are not only reliably associated with experiential determinables, but also highly specific with regard to experiential determinates, because they associate particular kinds of pain—that of a burning or dull quality, and that of a pricking or stinging quality—with the activity of particular types of nociceptive fibers (the former to C-, and the latter to A-Δ fibers).

However, they will be quick to remark that at exactly this stage of our knowledge of the specific psychophysical connec-tions, we have reached the point where the explanatory gap or the hard problems of consciousness impose themselves upon the theoretically demanding mind. For they will claim that, so far, no property of the relevant sensory fibers has been discovered that would show us that the tight connection between the firing of these fibers and pain experience is intelligible, and not just a matter of brute, unexplainable (untransparent) correlation. In other words, they will be convinced that no property has been disclosed that would in any way help us give satisfactory answers to the hard problems of consciousness related to the firing of A-Δ and C-nociceptive fibers: Why does their firing evoke pain, rather than some other sensation? Why does their firing evoke pain, rather than no sensation at all? Why does the firing of A-Δ nociceptive fibers elicit pricking or stinging pain, rather than dull or burning pain? Why does the firing of C-nociceptive fibers induce dull or burning pain, rather than pricking or stinging pain? Any satisfactory explanation, according to Levine, is a matter of removing alternatives:

I want to know why some event occurred, or why some object manifests a particular property; why this and not that.... That is, we must be able to see why if the explanation is true then the alternative events could not have occurred. Anything less leaves us explanatorily frustrated. (Levine 1991, p. 38)

So, if these explanatory demands are taken into account, it might well appear that what has been explained by the electrophysiological and psychophysical studies presented above is at most the causal role of pain: its functional property of being typically induced by noxious or potentially noxious stimuli. We now know, on the basis of strong electrophysiological and psychophysical evidence, that this role is performed by A-Δ and C-nociceptive fibers because these sensory units, unlike other sensory units, preferentially respond exactly to those stimuli which typically cause pain. However, it will be immediately pointed out, there is more to our concept of pain than its causal role:

There is its qualitative character, how it feels; and what is left unexplained by the discovery of C-fiber firing is why pain should feel the way it does! For there seems to be nothing about C-fiber firing which makes it naturally "fit" the phenomenal properties of pain, any more than it would fit some other set of phenomenal properties. Unlike its functional role, the identification of the qualitative side of pain with C-fiber firing (or some property of C-fiber firing) leaves the connection between it and what we identify it with completely mysterious. One might say, it makes the way pain feels into merely a brute fact. (Levine 1983, p. 357)

But to the theoretically naive and philosophically untroubled mind, it may well seem that—contrary to Levine—we have already discovered some things about C-fiber firing which makes it naturally "fit" the sensation of pain. For we have learned, on independent electrophysiological grounds (via the technique of intraneural microrecording of the activity of sensory fibers during the delivery of natural stimuli), that this firing is distinctively evoked by noxious or potentially noxious stimuli. Are these stimuli not considered adequate and appropriate for pain? Won't any definition of pain have to refer to them? Consider the definition of pain given by the IASP Subcommittee on Classification, and the comments that follow it:

An unpleasant sensory and emotional experience associated with actual or potential tissue damage, or described in terms of such damage.

Each individual learns the application of the word through the experience related to injury in early life. Biologists recognize that those stimuli which cause pain are liable to damage tissue. Accordingly, pain is that experience which we associate with actual or potential tissue damage. (IASP Subcommittee on Classification 1986, p. 217)

So, when we are informed, through the meticulous psychophysical studies which rely on the powerful and exquisitely precise technique of intraneural microstimulation, that there is a tight connection between the firing of C-nociceptive fibers and pain, it will (or at least should) seem to us that we can understand or explain that connection: the physiological specialization of these fibers, which consists in their preferential or distinctive responsiveness to noxious or potentially noxious stimuli, makes their connection to pain intelligible *because pain is exactly conceived by us as being distinctively evoked by such stimuli.* Thus, pain and the firing of C-nociceptive fibers share one distinctive property in common, and we can therefore see why they are tightly connected, or why the firing of these fibers naturally "fits" the sensation of pain and not some other sensation.

The underlying issue of the hard problem of consciousness is that of what makes something intelligible. Generally speaking, it seems that we are allowed to rely on something that is already intelligible to us in order to bestow intelligibility upon something that does not wear that mark or distinction on its sleeve. The intelligibility of the relationship between C-nociceptive fiber firing (as well as A-Δ nociceptive fiber firing) and pain is just such a conferred or second-order intelligibility, established via the first-order or conferring intelligibility of the functional-phenomenal relationship between noxious or potentially noxious stimuli and pain. If the relationship between pain and noxious stimuli is, as such, intelligible to us, the role of these stimuli as adequate or appropriate stimuli both for pain and for the activity of C- and A-Δ nociceptive fibers will imbue, through conceptual mediation, homogeneity between phenomenal and physiological concepts which are (thus far) normally thought to be inherently heterogeneous. Thus, conceptual heterogeneity or categorical difference between experiential and physical (neurophysiological) predicates will no longer feature as the main legitimate source for further explanatory demands with regard to the established psychophysical connections. In other words, the way will be opened for the theoretical integration of the experiential into the physical.

This answer to the "hard" problem in no way implies that the a priori analysis of phenomenal states in functional terms is a prerequisite for a satisfactory or adequate psychophysical explanation of qualia. The connection between noxious or potentially noxious stimuli and pain is, in a sense to be explained later, intelligible as such, and it will bestow intelligibility upon the connection between the firing of C- and A-Δ nociceptive fibers established by psychophysical studies, if it is found out through the relevant electrophysiological experiments that this firing is distinctively evoked exactly by those stimuli which are considered by us to be intelligibly attached to the experience of pain. Thus, the discovery that C- and A-Δ fibers distinctively or preferentially respond to noxious or potentially noxious stimuli will not only reveal to us neural structures that perform the causal role of pain, but will also lead us to see that there is an intelligible close connection between the firing of these fibers and pain experience. In other words, functionalist considerations of phenomenal states will play the role of hermeneutical mediators in psychophysical explanations, and not—as in Lewis's standard model (1966, pp. 17–25)—the role of aprioristic tools that are supposed to open the only way to adequate or satisfactory psychophysical explanations.

It might be objected that we have just postponed the hard problem of consciousness related to the connection between the firing of C- and A-Δ nociceptive fibers and pain; that we have merely relegated the problem to the functional-phenomenal level where it will be directed at the connection between noxious or potentially noxious stimuli and pain. For the further questions will now be: Why do these stimuli give rise to pain, and not to some other sensation? Why do they give rise to pain, rather than to no sensation at all? As Levine has remarked, "it still seems that we can ask why the kind of state that performs the function performed by pain, whatever its physical basis, should feel the way pain does" (Levine 1983, p. 358). A similar theoretical objection is found in Chalmers:

We know that conscious experience does arise when these functions are performed, but the very fact that it arises is the central mystery. There is an explanatory gap . . . between the functions and experience, and we need an explanatory bridge to cross it. (Chalmers 1995, p. 203)

If no satisfactory reply can be given to the demands for further intelligibility between certain functions and the experience of pain, this will certainly cast doubt on the conferred or second-order intelligibility of the connection between the firing of nociceptive fibers and pain, and we will be back to square one as far as an adequate explanation of this psychophysical connection is concerned. It is at this point that conceivability arguments (in either the inverted or absent qualia version) will be introduced in order to prove that no such satisfactory replies are forthcoming or, in principle, are to be expected. For if we can easily and clearly conceive, as it is supposed by these arguments, that noxious or potentially noxious stimulation of some part of our body is not followed by pain, but by some other sensation or no sensation at all, this will be taken as a reliable signal of the presence of the explanatory gap—the nonintelligibility of the relationship between such stimuli and pain.

But it is not as clear as it might first appear that the demand for further intelligibility is appropriate when considering the relationship between certain functional and phenomenal properties of pain. Likewise, it is not at all obvious that in the case of such relationships, conceivability arguments have the epistemic force and import that Levine is attributing to them. As far as the connection between the functional and phenomenal properties of pain is concerned, the first thing to notice is that the pull toward the demand for further intelligibility or explanation of this connection is not, or should not be, as strong as it is in the case of the psychophysical correlation between the firing of certain neural structures and pain. The reason is that in the former case, there is no conceptual heterogeneity or categorical difference between functional and phenomenal predicates that would make that demand seem immediately appropriate or understandable. On the contrary, functional properties are assumed to naturally go with phenomenal states, which is proved by the fact that they are regularly referred to in definitions of these states; as a rule they feature in all our conceptions of such states. In fact, some relations between physical properties or magnitudes (for instance, the relationship between mass and distance captured by the gravitational constant) are taken for granted or considered not to be in need of further explanation, because they fit smoothly into our theory of the physical or form a part of the same family, the same overall system of description.

However, it seems that the pull toward the demand for further intelligibility is not only less strong in the case of the association of the functional and phenomenal properties of pain, but that it is in principle directed more at cases of real or possible disassociation of these properties than at their association. One might argue that in this sense, the demand for further explanation or understanding of the relationship between noxious or potentially noxious stimuli and pain (or, to use more familiar terms, between injury and pain) would be inappropriate. As far as the intelligibility of this relationship is concerned, the proper question is not *why* injury elicits pain, but rather *how* it is possible for injury not to be followed by pain, as well as for pain to appear without injury. What cries out for explanation and where the requirement for adequate theory is most pressing are exactly the cases of the dissociation between pain and injury. To support this contention, it suffices to say that in pain research and theory, out of seven of the most puzzling facts that are considered to require explanation by any new or adequate model of pain, four are related to the dissociation of pain from injury:

(1) the relationship between pain and injury is highly variable; (2) innocuous stimuli may produce pain; (3) the location of pain may be different from the location of damage; (4) pain may persist in the absence of injury or after healing. (Melzack and Wall 1988, p. 165)

That an injury, even a severe one, is not regularly followed by pain has been proved by clinical evidence. For example, 37 percent of patients who arrived at an emergency clinic with a variety of serious injuries "stated that they did not feel pain at the time of injury. The majority of these patients reported onset of pain within an hour of injury, although the delays were as long as 9 hours in some patients" (Melzack, Wall, and Ty 1982, p. 33). On the other hand, there are cases of pain where no injury is involved: for example, it is reported that "as many as 60–78 percent of patients who suffer low back pain have no apparent physical signs" (Melzack and Wall 1988, p. 58). "Gentle touch, vibration, and other non-noxious stimuli can trigger excruciating pain" (ibid., p. 75) in causalgia and the neuralgias, and pain from hyperalgesic areas of the skin often arises after long delays and continues long after the removal of the

stimulus. The clinical data also show that there can be a mismatch between the site of injury and the site of pain exempli-
fied in cases of referred or transferred pain found in patients
with appendicitis and angina pectoris. Furthermore, in many
cases of chronic pain, intense, debilitating pain persists for
months or even years after all possible healing has been com-
pleted; and this pain, in contrast to acute pain, "is no longer
the symptom of a disease but becomes a serious medical syndrome that requires attention for its own sake" (ibid., p. 12).

When presented with such cases of the dissociation or mismatch between pain and injury, we will immediately think of
them as puzzling or mysterious, as something that demands
explanation. But that would not be the case if the very relationship between pain and injury seemed to us to be puzzling
or mysterious. For us, the mark of the intelligibility of that relationship is found in the fact that the cases of the dissociation
of pain from injury cry out for explanation; they are considered
deeply puzzling or mysterious. As we have already noted, in that
sense, the demand for further explanation of the relationship
between pain and injury would be inappropriate. Generally
speaking, the inappropriateness of these demands will critically
depend on whether the pull toward such demands (the per-
plexity ratio) is directed more at the dissociations than at the
associations of the functional and phenomenal properties of the
mental states under consideration.

For Levine, and philosophers who share his interpretation of
the explanatory gap problem, the conceivability of the dissociation between functional and phenomenal properties of a
certain mental state is to be taken as a reliable mark of the nonintelligibility of their linkage. In the case that we are interested
in, this would mean that we can pry apart in imagination pain

and injury—conceive them as appearing one without the other—exactly because they seem to us to be arbitrarily stacked together; because the nonintelligibility of their relationship underlies or is the proper source of the apparent contingency of their connection. If that was not so, we could not so easily and clearly imagine injury without the feeling of pain, as well as pain without injury. I will not discuss the question of whether we can really so easily and clearly imagine this state of affairs, but will rather concentrate on the intelligibility issues related to that which we are supposed to imagine: the absence of pain in the presence of severe injury. Imagine, for this purpose, that a needle has been severely pricked in the fingertip of our physical and functional doppelgänger (conceived as much as possible in its full flesh and blood), or that he has pressed his fingertip against a hot electric lightbulb, but that he feels no pain.

Assuming that we can clearly imagine this state of affairs, we will certainly be amazed by what we have imagined; we will immediately ask ourselves how it is possible and will regard the demand for further explanation as fully appropriate. If imagined cases of the dissociation of pain from injury will be regarded by us as something that is perplexing, puzzling, or mysterious, the fact that we can conceive such state of affairs will not signal—contrary to Levine—the presence of an explanatory gap; it will not reveal the unintelligibility of the connection between pain and injury and thus will not show that the demand for further explanation of this connection is appropriate. That we can conceive injury without pain as well as pain without injury is rather to be explained by the simple fact that they are, to use traditional terminology, distinct existences. As Hume long ago remarked, whatever is distinct is separable in mind and imagination. But this does not mean that pain and injury are arbitrarily stacked together; that their relationship is mysterious or unintelligible because we do not see at all why they should be tightly connected. It speaks only against the identification of pain with injury and merely shows that pain cannot be a priori analyzed in terms of its causal role as is attempted in the so-called perceptual view or model of pain. The general lesson to be learned from these considerations is that the a priori analysis of phenomenal concepts in functional terms is not a prerequisite for adequate or intelligible psychophysical explanations. Moreover, it turns out that conceivability considerations are actually a poor guide for the assessment of the intelligibility or adequacy of such explanations.

One might complain that the experimentally induced dull or burning pain elicited by the electrical stimulation of C-fibers shows that the distinctive responsiveness of these fibers to the damaging or potentially damaging stimuli is not something that grounds (makes sensible or intelligible) their connection to the experience of pain. For in this case, there is, indeed, a strong connection between the firing of the relevant kind of fibers and pain, although that activity was not induced by damaging or potentially damaging stimuli. But notice that, in these cases, there still exists the perfect or very close match between the projected field of the sensation (the site where the artificially induced pain is felt) and the receptive field of C-fibers (the site or innervation territory where natural noxious stimuli instigate their activity). If that is the case, the role of damaging or potentially damaging stimulation as the intelligible bridging property has been preserved. Owing to the role of C-fibers in locognosia, instead of loosening the tie between pain and injury, the cases under consideration seem to tighten it in a quite unexpected way.

The intelligibility of the relationship between the firing of C-fibers and pain (conferred or second-order intelligibility), established via the intelligibility of the functional-phenomenal relationship between injury and pain (conferring or first-order intelligibility), will provide an answer to the two "hard" problems of consciousness related to pain: Why does C-fiber firing evoke pain, and not some other kind of sensation? Why does it evoke any sensation at all? An answer to the third "hard" problem of consciousness related to the physiological grounds of the qualitative differences between various kinds of pain— why does C-fiber firing give rise to dull and not sharp pain?— is to be sought in the different physical modes of activity of C-fibers and other fibers responsible for pain. In other words, the physical (neurophysiological) explanation of sensory determinables (intermodal differences) will have to rely on the functional properties common to certain phenomenal states and corresponding neural structures, while sensory determinates (intramodal differences) will have a more direct neurophysiological account. When we are looking for such explanations of the qualitative differences between experiential determinates, we will have to search for property affinities between some features of the relevant neural structures and qualitative characteristics of the corresponding phenomenal states. For instance, the conspicuous difference in conduction velocities between A-Δ and C-fibers, as well as the fact of the ongoing activity of C-fibers after stimulation, could explain in terms of property affinities why the former kind of fibers give rise to sharp pain, while the latter kind of fibers give rise to dull pain. Within our general theoretical framework, the really hard problem will be to explain the functional properties that are characteristic of certain neural structures through the morphological properties of these structures. For example: why do C-fibers and A-Δ fibers preferentially respond to noxious or potentially noxious stimuli, and not to some other kind of stimuli? Although we do not yet have answers to these questions, and are thus with respect to them at the "ignoramus" stage, it seems that they are not of such a kind which must lead us to "ignoramibus" despair.

References

Adrian, E. D. (1931). "The Messages in Sensory Nerve Fibres after Their Interpretation." *Proceedings of the Royal Society B* 109:1–18.

Barber, T. X. (1959). "Toward a Theory of Pain: Relief of Chronic Pain by Prefrontal Leucotomy, Opiates, Placebos, and Hypnosis." *Psychological Bulletin* 56:430–460.

Bentham, J. (1948). *An Introduction to the Principles of Morals and Legislation.* New York: Hafner.

Berthier, M., Starkstein, S., and Leiguarda, R. (1988). "Pain Asymbolia: A Sensory-Limbic Disconnection Syndrome." *Annals of Neurology* 24: 41–49.

Biemond, A. (1956). "The Conduction of Pain above the Level of the Thalamus Opticus." *Archives of Neurology and Psychiatry* 75:221–231.

Brand, P., and Yancey, P. (1997). *The Gift of Pain* (previously titled *The Gift Nobody Wants*). Michigan: Zondervan Publishing House.

Burgess, P. R., and Perl, E. R. (1973). "Cutaneous Mechano-receptors and Nociceptors." In *Somato-sensory System, Handbook of Sensory Physiology*, vol. I, edited by A. Iggo, pp. 29–79. Berlin: Springer-Verlag.

Campbell, K. (1983). "Abstract Particulars and the Philosophy of Mind." *Australasian Journal of Philosophy* 61:129–141.

Chalmers, D. (1995). "Facing Up to the Problem of Consciousness." *Journal of Consciousness Studies* 2:200–219.

Chapman, R. C., and Nakamura, Y. (1999). "A Passion of the Soul: An Introduction to Pain for Consciousness Researchers." *Consciousness and Cognition* 8:391–422.

Chapman, R. C., Nakamura, Y., and Flores, L. Y. (2000). "How We Hurt: A Constructivist Framework for Understanding Individual Differences in Pain." In *Individual Differences in Conscious Experience,* edited by R. G. Kunzendorf and B. Wallace, pp. 17–44. Amsterdam: John Benjamin.

Chapman, W. P., Solomon, H. C., and Rose, A. S. (1950). "Measurements of Motor Withdrawal Reaction in Patients Following Frontal Lobotomy." In *Studies in Lobotomy,* edited by M. Greenblat, R. Arnot, and H. C. Solomon, pp. 386–392. New York: Grune & Straton.

Churchland, Paul, and Churchland, Patricia (1981). "Functionalism, Qualia, and Intentionality." *Philosophical Topics* 12:121–145.

Cleeland, C. S., Nakamura, Y., Howland, E. W., Morgan, N. R., Edwards, K. R., and Backonja, M. (1996). "Effects of Oral Morphine on Cold Pressor Tolerance Time and Neuropsychological Performance." *Neuropsychopharmacology* 15:252–262.

Coghill, R. C., Sang, C. N., Maisog, J. M., and Iadarola, M. A. (1999). "Pain Intensity Processing within the Human Brain: A Bilateral, Distributed Mechanism." *Journal of Neurophysiology* 82:1934–1943.

Cohen, R. A., Kaplan, R. F., Zuffante, P., Moser, D. J., Jenkins, M. A., Salloway, S., and Wilkinson, H. (1999). "Alteration of Intention and Self-Initiated Action Associated With Bilateral Anterior Cingulotomy." *Journal of Neuropsychiatry and Clinical Neuroscience* 11:444–453.

Critchley, M. (1956). "Congenital Indifference to Pain." *Annals of Internal Medicine* 45:737–747.

Dearborn, G. (1932). "A Case of Congenital General Pure Analgesia." *Journal of Nervous and Mental Diseases* 75:612–615.

Dennett, D. C. (1978). "Why You Can't Make a Computer That Feels Pain." *Synthese* 38:415–456.

Denny-Brown, D. (1962). "Clinical Symptomology in Right and Left Hemispheric Lesions." In *Intrahemispheric Relations and Cerebral*

Dominance, edited by V. B. Mountcastle, pp. 244–252. Baltimore: The Johns Hopkins University Press.

Descartes, R. (1968). *The Philosophical Works of Descartes,* vol. I. Edited and translated by E. S. Haldane and G. R. T. Ross. Cambridge: Cambridge University Press.

Dong, W. K., Chudler, E. H., Sugiyama, K., Roberts, V. J., and Hayashi, T. (1994). "Somatosensory, Multi-sensory, and Task-Related Neurons in Cortical Area 7b (PF) of Unanesthetized Monkeys." *Journal of Neurophysiology* 72:542–564.

Dong, W. K., Hayashi, T., Roberts, V. J., Fusco, B. M., and Chudler, E. H. (1996). "Behavioral Outcome of Posterior Parietal Cortex Injury in the Monkey." *Pain* 64:579–587.

Foltz, E. L., and White, L. E. (1962). "Pain 'Relief' by Frontal Cingulotomy." *Journal of Neurosurgery* 19:89–100.

Freeman, W., and Watts, J. W. (1950). *Psychosurgery in the Treatment of Mental Disorders and Intractable Pain,* second edition. Oxford: Blackwell.

Geschwind, N. (1965). "Disconnexion Syndromes in Animals and Man. Part I." *Brain* 88:237–294.

Greenspan, J. D., Lee, R. R., and Lenz, F. A. (1999). "Pain Sensitivity as a Function of Lesion Location in the Parasylvian Cortex." *Pain* 81:273–282.

Hall, K. R. L., and Stride, E. (1954). "The Varying Response to Pain in Psychiatry Disorders." *British Journal of Medical Psychology* 27:48–60.

Halligan, P. W., Marshall, J. C., Hunt, M., and Wade, D. T. (1997). "Somatosensory Assessment: Can Seeing Produce Feeling?" *Journal of Neurology* 244:190–203.

Hardcastle, V. (1999). *The Myth of Pain.* Cambridge, Mass.: MIT Press.

Hardy, J. D., Wolff, H. G., and Goodel, H. (1952). *Pain Sensations and Reactions.* New York: Hafner.

Head, H. (1920). *Studies in Neurology.* London: Frowde, Hodder, and Stoughton.

Hemphill, R. E., and Stengel, E. (1940). "A Study on Pure Word-Deafness." *Journal of Neurology and Psychiatry* 3:251–262.

Hoogenraad, T. U., Ramos, L. M., and van Gijn, J. (1994). "Visually Induced Central Pain and Arm Withdrawal after Right Parietal Infarction." *Journal of Neurology, Neurosurgery, and Psychiatry* 57:850–852.

Hutchison, W. D., Davis, K. D., Lozano, A. M., Tasker, R. R., and Dostrovsky, J. O. (1999). "Pain-related Neurons in the Human Cingulate Cortex." *Nature Neuroscience* 2:403–405.

International Association for the Study of Pain (IASP) Subcommittee on Classification (1986). "Pain Terms: A Current List with Definitions and Notes on Usage." *Pain*, Supplement 3:216–221.

Levine, J. (1983). "Materialism and Qualia: The Explanatory Gap Problem." *Pacific Philosophical Quarterly* 64:354–361.

Levine, J. (1991). "Cool Red." *Philosophical Psychology* 4:27–40.

Lewis, D. (1966). "An Argument for the Identity Theory." *Journal of Philosophy* 63:17–25.

Lewis, D. (1995). "Should a Materialist Believe in Qualia?" *Australasian Journal of Philosophy* 73:140–144.

Masson, C., Koskas, P., Cambier, J., and Masson, M. (1991). "Syndrome cortical pseudothalamique gauche et asymbolie à la douleur." *Revue Neurologique* 10:668–670.

McMahon, S. B., and Koltzenburg, M. (1990). "Novel Classes of Nociceptors: Beyond Sherrington." *Trends in Neurosciences* (June): 254–255.

McMurray, G. A. (1955). "Congenital Insensitivity to Pain and Its Implications for Motivational Theory." *Canadian Journal of Psychology* 9:121–131.

Melzack, R., and Wall, P. (1989). *The Challenge of Pain*. Harmondsworth: Penguin Books.

Melzack, R., Wall, P. D., and Ty, T. C. (1982). "Acute Pain in an Emergency Clinic: Latency of Onset and Descriptor Patterns Related to Different Injuries." *Pain* 14:33–43.

Mesulam, M. M., and Mufson, E. (1985). "The Insula of Reil in Man and Monkey. Architectonics, Connectivity and Function." In *Cerebral Cortex*, vol. 4, edited by A. Peters and E. G. Jones, pp. 179–226. New York: Plenum.

Millan, M. J. (1999). "The Induction of Pain: An Integrative Review." *Progress in Neurobiology* 57:1–164.

Mitchell, S. W. (1872). *Injuries of Nerves and Their Consequences.* Philadelphia: J. B. Lippincott.

Nelkin, N. (1994). "Reconsidering Pain." *Philosophical Psychology* 7:325–343.

Ochoa, J., and Torebjörk, E. (1983). "Sensations Evoked by Intraneural Microstimulation of Single Mechanoreceptor Units Innervating the Human Hand." *Journal of Physiology* 342:633–665.

Ochoa, J., and Torebjörk, E. (1989). "Sensations Evoked by Intraneural Microstimulation of C Nociceptor Fibers in Human Skin Nerves." *Journal of Physiology* 415:583–599.

Perl, E. R. (1984). "Characterization of Nociceptors and Their Activation of Neurons in the Superficial Dorsal Horn: First Step for the Sensation of Pain." In *Advances in Pain Research and Therapy*, vol. 6, edited by L. Kruger and J. C. Liebeskind, pp. 23–51. New York: Raven Press.

Pitcher, G. (1970). "Pain Perception." *Philosophical Review* 79:368–393.

Ploner, M., Freund, H.-J., and Schnitzler, A. (1999). "Pain Affect without Pain Sensation in a Patient with a Postcentral Lesion." *Pain* 81:211–214.

Pötzl, O., and Stengel, E. (1937). "Über das Syndrom Leitungsaphasie-Schmerzasymbolie." *Jahrbuch der Psychiatrie* 53:174–207.

Price, D. D. (2000). "Psychological and Neural Mechanisms of the Affective Dimension of Pain." *Science* 288:1769–1772.

Price, D. D., and Dubner, R. (1977). "Neurons That Subserve the Sensory-Discriminative Aspects of Pain." *Pain* 3:307–338.

Ramachandran, V. S. (1998). "Consciousness and Body Image: Lessons from Phantom Limbs, Capgras Syndrome, and Pain Asymbolia."

Philosophical Transactions of the Royal Society of London—Series B: Biological Sciences 353:1851–1859.

Robinson, C. J., and Burton, H. (1980). "Somatic Submodality Distribution within the Second Somatosensory (SII). 7b, Retroinsula, Postauditory and Granular Insula of *M. fascicularis.*" *Journal of Comparative Neurology* 192:93–108.

Rubins, J. L., and Friedman, E. D. (1948). "Pain Asymbolia." *Archives of Neurology and Psychiatry* 60:554–573.

Ryle, G. (1973). *The Concept of Mind.* Harmondsworth: Penguin.

Schilder, P., and Stengel, E. (1928). "Schmerzasymbolie." *Zeitschrift für die gesamte Neurologie und Psychiatrie* 113:143–148.

Sherrington, C. (1900). "Cutaneous Sensations." In *Textbook of Physiology,* edited by E. A. Schäfer, pp. 920–1001. London: Pentland.

Sherrington, C. (1948). *The Integrative Action of the Nervous System* (originally published in 1906). Cambridge: Cambridge University Press.

Sinclair, D. C. (1967). *Cutaneous Sensation.* Oxford: Oxford University Press.

Talbot, J. D., Villemure, J.-G., Bushnell, M. C., and Duncan, G. H. (1995). "Evaluation of Pain Perception after Anterior Capsulotomy: A Case Report." *Somatosensory and Motor Research* 12:115–126.

Torebjörk, E., and Ochoa, J. (1980). "Specific Sensations Evoked by Activity in Single Identified Sensory Units in Man." *Acta Physiologica Scandinavica* 110:445–447.

Torebjörk, E., Vallbo, A. B., and Ochoa, J. (1987). "Intraneural Microstimulation in Man." *Brain* 110:1509–1529.

Trelles, J. O. (1978). "Asimbolia al dolor." *Revista Neuropsiquiatrica* 41:3–20.

Trigg, R. (1970). *Pain and Emotion.* Oxford: Clarendon Press.

Tye, M. (1989). *The Metaphysics of Mind.* Cambridge: Cambridge University Press.

Tye, M. (1995). *Ten Problems of Consciousness.* Cambridge, Mass.: MIT Press.

Vallbo, A. B., and Hagbarth, K. E. (1968). "Activity from Skin Mechanoreceptors Recorded Percutaneously in Awake Human Subjects." *Experimental Neurology* 21:270–289.

Wade, J. B., Dougherty, L. M., Archer, C. R., and Price, D. D. (1996). "Assessing the Stages of Pain Processing: A Multivariate Analytical Approach." *Pain* 68:157–167.

Wall, P. (1999). *Pain: The Science of Suffering.* London: Weidenfeld & Nicolson.

Wall, P. D., and McMahon, S. B. (1985). "Microneurography and Its Relation to Perceived Sensation: A Critical Review." *Pain* 21:209–229.

Weinstein, E. A., Kahn, R. L., and Slote, W. H. (1955). "Withdrawal, Inattention, and Pain Asymbolia." *Archives of Neurology and Psychiatry* 74:235–248.

Wittgenstein, L. (1968). *Philosophical Investigations.* Oxford: Basil Blackwell.

Index

A-β thermoreceptors, 12
"Absent qualia" argument,
    76–77, 159
Acquired analgesia. *See*
    Congenital analgesia
Acute pain, 12
A-Δ nociceptive fibers
    avoidance system role of, 11–13
    C-fibers vs., 144
    conduction velocity of, 11, 144,
    165
    description of, 11n, 143–144
    pain concept and, 157–158
    pain types associated with, 11,
    143, 165
    philosophers on, 141, 154–155
    physiological properties of,
    143–148
    stimuli of, 145–147, 166
    study methods for, 144–145,
    148–150
Affective-cognitive dimension of
    pain. *See also* Painfulness
    without pain

absence of, 52, 61–65, 81–82
evolutionary value of, 81
lobotomy and, 131–137
sensation of pain vs.
    significance of pain as object of
    reaction, 133–137
significance of, for
    understanding pain, 40, 80–82
Anterior cingulate cortex, 21, 32,
    91
Anterior insula, 64
Anterior insular cortex, 91
Antirealism, 102
Antisubjectivism, 103–107
Approach behavior to pain, 36,
    45–46, 71
Area 7b, 56–61, 65, 68–70
Avoidance system
    neural structures of, 10–13
    pain asymbolia and, 47–48
    role of, 9–10

Behavior. *See* Pain behavior
Behaviorism, 39